RUM

RUM

Dave Broom

Photographs by Jason Lowe

Mitchell Beazley

Rum
by Dave Broom

First published in Great Britain in 2003
by Mitchell Beazley, an imprint of Octopus
Publishing Group Ltd, 2–4 Heron Quays,
London E14 4JP

A CIP catalogue record for this book is available
from the British Library.

ISBN 1 84000 730 3

Photographs by Jason Lowe
Illustration by Neil Gower

Commissioning Editor: Hilary Lumsden
Executive Art Editor: Yasia Williams
Design: Grade Design Consultants, London
Managing Editor: Emma Rice
Editor: Jamie Ambrose
Assistant Editor: Juanne Branquinho
Index: Ann Parry
Production: Alexis Coogan

Typeset in Serifa

Printed and bound by Toppan Printing Company
in China

Dedicated to my darling bairn, Rosie
"May the long time sun shine upon you, all love
surround you, and the pure light within you guide
your way on."

**Mitchell Beazley would like to give particular
thanks to:**

Wray & Nephew and John Hammond at
Hammond & Deacon;
Havana Club and Charlotte Fraser at Richmond
Towers, and Pernod-Ricard UK;
Clément and Patrik Goasdoué;
St Lucia Distillers Ltd and Katherine Felix

for their support in sponsoring the photoshoot for
this book in the Caribbean. We also extend our
thanks to everyone based with the companies in
the Caribbean for the generosity, hospitality and
assistance offered to the author, Dave Broom and
photographer, Jason Lowe.

Photography:
The Publisher acknowledges that the photography
contained throughout this book will not always
correspond to the text contained in the section in
which the photograph appears.

Rum labels:
Mitchell Beazley has made every effort to contact
the producers of the rums whose labels are
illustrated in this book.
Mitchell Beazley would also like to thank Petr
Hlousek for his help with supplying labels for
the book.

Contents

Introduction

Rum has been the forgotten spirit. Here is a drink that has been the catalyst for the birth of nations. It helped create capitalism and thereby colonialism and it is still there, centre stage, as we move into a globalized world. Rum people have been slavers, pirates, and smugglers as well as artists, blenders, and barmen. Rum was slavery's currency; it made some people vast fortunes and helped others forget their misery. It gave sailors and soldiers courage in battle; was at the heart of Prohibition and, in recent years, it has been at the centre of international trade wars. It has also become central to a Caribbean sense of place and self. No other spirit comes close to that. Yet this rum tale is one that few know – and fewer still have been allowed to tell.

That's why I wanted to write this book: that and the fact it also tastes bloody great! (Rum, that is, not the book.) The writing of this tale has taken me around the Caribbean and into South America as well as closer to home: to Glasgow, London, Bristol, and Amsterdam. It has made me happy, sad, and angry, and filled me with hope for the future of this remarkable drink. I've sipped cocktails in Havana, limed (hung out) in Guyana, sampled Carnival in Trinidad, and met generous, talented people who have spent their working lives creating some of the finest spirits you will ever taste.

The result is not a guide to every distillery or every rum. What it is, hopefully, is a taste of where rum came from, where it is made, where it is going, and why it tastes the way it does.

No other spirit can make you quite so happy in just being alive. All human life is contained, genie-like, within that bottle in front of you. One sniff and you are transported into a new, sweeter dimension filled with spices, honey, citrus and tropical fruits. Shut your eyes and you can hear the sound of the sea caressing the white sand. Rum is seductive. But it has much more to give.

When you taste a great rum, you don't just think of what it tastes like, but how and why those flavours were put there. Enter this world and you will soon find that there is no such thing as "rum". It is diverse, multi-faceted. Every island has its own style, every country has its own flavour, and every distillery has a variation on each. Rum speaks of its place. Its history is one of displacement, emigration, and creation: of a new drink, of new aromas and flavours, of new societies, of new ways of doing business.

Rum was born in pain. "Like sugar," said my Guyanan friend Zadok, serious for one moment, "it is tainted with the brush of slavery." That, of course, is inescapable. Yet today, at long last, rum is being reborn into joy. Which is just as it should be, for rum is a drink unlike any other. It fuels laughter and good times, helps you shake off your inhibitions and throw yourself into the sheer joy of life.

Rum is hip at the moment, but unlike other marketing-driven fads, it can grow on the back of its new-found fashionability. Why? Because it doesn't just have a range of flavours and styles; it can draw on its fantastic, bloody, passionate history: just as malt whisky has, just as Cognac has. Rum has flavour, it has heritage, and it has quality. Vitally, its future is now in the hands of the people who best understand this: the rum-makers of the Caribbean and South America, who can see a new quality era for the spirit.

In the twenty-first century, rum is no longer forgotten. Rum has come home.

History of Rum

It all started with a plant – a grass, in fact – known to botanists as *Saccharum officinarum* and to the rest of us as sugar cane, which was first cultivated in New Guinea some 10,000 years ago. By 6,000 BC, it was being grown in Indonesia, the Philippines, and India. What was it used for? Not rum, that's certain, but written evidence shows that, by 350 BC in India, sugar cane was being used to make sugar and fermented drinks. Around this time, Nearchus, Alexander the Great's general, reported that, on a journey from the River Indus to the River Euphrates, he had come into contact with "an Indian reed [which] brings forth honey without the help of bees, from which an intoxicating drink is made". The fact that there were Indian words, *gaudi* and *sidhu*, for fermented sugar drinks, suggests that this is what Nearchus may have tried. Man has always had a sweet tooth. Now here was a magical plant that could be cultivated easily and gave a product similar to honey, but in greater quantities – and with less risk of bee stings.

By the seventh century, sugar cane had begun its westward march and passed into the hands of the Arabs. As their empire spread into Cyprus, Malta, and Sicily, across the north African coast and into Spain and Portugal, sugar cane followed. The Moors not only brought with them a new religion, but advances in science and agriculture – and, therefore, sugar production.

Sugar wasn't a lump of white stuff to drop in tea or coffee but an expensive spice which could be used in cooking and, more importantly, as a medicine. There is no evidence that Arab scholars made a potable spirit, but they did understand the art of distillation. Our words "alcohol" and "alembic" are Arabic, products of that hermetic science called *al-khem*, or as we know it, alchemy.

Arabic schools of medicine used sugar to sweeten their concoctions. It was also used for medicinal purposes, as the base for many rather pleasant-sounding remedies: *shurba*, or sherberts; *rubb* (robb) – fruits and flowers immersed in syrup; and *gulab* – rosewater with sugar, which translates as our julep (we'll meet that one again).

Yet sugar wasn't solely medicinal. It was becoming a symbol of wealth and power, and as nation states emerged in the fifteenth century, so control of sugar production became increasingly desirable. By then, the Portuguese and Spanish had begun to explore the African coastline and in order to protect their trade, they established colonies on the Canary Islands, Madeira, and São Tomé. By 1450, these islands were supplying the bulk of Europe's sugar, which, in a manner that has continued to the present day, was produced there and sent either to Antwerp or London to be refined. Sugar was still considered a spice, and the Dutch and English were vying for control of that lucrative trade.

The Portuguese and Spanish had bigger ideas. They desired spices, but they also wanted gold. In front of them was an ocean leading to the riches of the east. Or at least that's what Christopher Columbus thought…

Planters, empires, and respectability

Columbus may not have discovered the East Indies on his first voyage, but the lands he found were worthy of exploration – and exploitation. On his second voyage (1493), his flotilla included sugar-cane growers from the Canaries, complete with vines which they planted on the island of Hispaniola. Other islands, such as Puerto Rico (1508), Jamaica (1509), and Cuba (1511) were soon settled by the Spanish. Although sugar cane was always planted, the chief aim was to mine for gold and other precious metals.

The Portuguese, however, saw the potential for sugar, and had begun establishing plantations in Brazil, using enslaved African workers and plying them with a fermented drink, known as *garapa doida* ("crazy sugar-cane juice"). By 1625, Brazil was supplying most of Europe's sugar. Did they distil it? Not initially. Commercial distilling was not yet fully developed in Europe. Only once that happened could sugar planters start importing their stills and start making rum.

The Caribbean sugar machine

In the early seventeenth century, the "sugar rush" was set to expand dramatically. In 1624, the English and French settled the island of St Kitts. The two nations rapidly seized most of the non-Spanish islands and, with the Dutch, employed privateers, corsairs, and buccaneers to harry the Spanish fleets. For sixty years, these mercenaries fought against the Spanish under any flag of convenience. They were stateless people: social misfits, convicts, and adventurers loyal only to each other. Bound by a tight moral and social code, they also acted as the islands' protectors. Take Jamaica, for example, which the English had seized in 1655. One of buccaneers' leaders, Henry Morgan, used his booty to buy a sugar plantation on the island; eventually, Captain Morgan, pirate, became Sir Henry Morgan, Jamaica's deputy governor.

As the English and French presence grew stronger, Portuguese control over the sugar industry began to weaken. By 1650, the British (in Barbados) and French (on Martinique) had established the plantation system. The Caribbean was about to become a massive sugar-making factory and rum distillery. By 1655, Barbados was the region's major producer of sugar, with an annual crop valued at £3 million. The British, French, and Portuguese all recognized sugar's potential as a commodity. Why, then, couldn't even more money be made by distilling the molasses that was effectively a syrupy waste product of the sugar-manufacturing process?

Let Sir Dalby Thomas, plantation owner, historian, and governor of Jamaica in 1690, explain. "We must consider, too," he wrote in an early work, "the Spirits arising from Melasses which is sent

Above: The planters built themselves elegant abodes, like this one in Martinique.

from the Sugar Colonies to the other Colonies and to England, which, if it were all… turned into spirits, would amount annually to above £500,000 at half the Price the like Quantity of Brandy from France would cost." Cane spirit had become a money-maker.

It had also been given a name – or, more precisely, names. To many, it was *eau-de-vie* or *aguardiente*, but the Portuguese called it *cachaça*, the Spanish *berbaje*, the people of Martinique knew it as *guildhive*, the English as *kill-devil* or *rumbullion*, and, according to one unknown source, it was "a hot, hellish, and terrible liquor".

Writing in Guadeloupe in 1696, French missionary Père Labat agreed. "The eau-de-vie… is very strong… has a disagreeable smell and a bitter taste… which one has difficulty in removing." This isn't rum as we know it. It is a burnt, oily spirit, badly made. "Hot and hellish" is pretty accurate.

The best account of early rum-making comes from Englishman Richard Ligon's story of life in Barbados, written in 1647. Among his vivid descriptions is a lengthy discourse of the workings of a sugar mill, complete with plan: the first drawing of a rum stillhouse. It was roughly twelve feet by ten, a building tacked on to the back of the sugar mill. There were two stills and a large cistern acting as a fermenter.

As for distillation, Ligon allows it a paragraph. The skilled part, the important part, was the production of sugar; rum was an after-thought. Although double distillation was being practised, this was a brutally strong spirit that had a tendency to catch fire when exposed to a naked flame. Early rum distillers weren't experienced. They bought a still by mail-order and relied on intuition. They weren't making a fine spirit. They were distilling a waste product, quickly, to make money.

From cure-all to cocktails

In its earliest incarnation, rum was a local drink made for indentured servants and slaves. Brandy and Madeira were the drinks for a civilized, superior gentleman planter. By contrast, rum was

a cure-all, a medicine, a liquid so potent it could numb pain and obliterate misery. That's not to say that the plantation owners didn't have the odd tipple – even if just for medicinal purposes and only, as Ligon suggests, if brandy or "English spirits" weren't available.

Quite when more care began to be taken over rum is hard to pin down, but it would have been motivated by the planters' realization that a better-quality spirit would attract a higher price. Certainly at the end of the seventeenth century, the English market had yet to acquire a taste for it. In 1698, for example, a scant 207 gallons of rum were imported. Yet less than a hundred years later, over two million gallons were arriving every year. By this time, rum was no longer hot and hellish; rum was fashionable.

This metamorphosis came about through an interplay between business and politics, and a natural evolution of skill. For starters, the art of distilling became better understood. Almost a hundred years after Ligon described his primitive stillhouse, *The Complete Distiller* by "A. Cooper" (1757) provided considerable details, not just about rum distillation but also about what was wrong with it. The author complained about the "stinky flavour" of the spirit:

> *It would be easy to rectify [further distil] the spirit and bring it to a much greater degree of purity for it brings over… a large amount of oil and this is often so disagreeable that the rum must be suffered to lie a long time to mellow before it can be used… If the business of rectifying rum was more nicely managed, it seems a very practical scheme to throw out so much of the oil as to reduce it to the fine, light state of clear spirit but lightly impregnated with the oil.*

Apart from showing that the science of wood-aging was unknown, this passage points to the fact that rums were still too flavoursome – *i.e.* badly distilled. Rum sales were rising, however, the direct result of the sugar boom. As the British

and French West Indies moved into mass production during the eighteenth century, sugar's price fell and consumption rose. Rum followed suit. Britain imported 1.6 million gallons in 1764 and roughly two million per year from then until the beginning of the nineteenth century.

In addition, British spirit was being distilled in London and Bristol from molasses – and plenty was being smuggled besides. Rum had been the beneficiary when the English grain harvest failed in 1699, and distillers had to import larger volumes of molasses initially used in gin production. The same thing happened in 1757. Once again, molasses – and, by now rum – grew on the back of a failed harvest. Rum thus became respectable. The punch bowl was being filled to overflowing.

The passion for punch

It isn't clear why or exactly where the trend for rum punch started. It could have been mere fashion, copying the manners of the rich planters, but I suspect it came down to the fact that it was a big jump from wine or Madeira to "stinky" rum. Diluting it cut the spirit's strong flavour; spicing it up masked some of its aromas. Whatever the reason, rum punch became an international craze. In Britain it also became decidedly middle-class. While the masses in England drank staggering amounts of gin, their betters quaffed punch made with the finest Jamaican or Barbadian rums.

The boom in sugar rum production bound the Caribbean colonies ever more tightly to their respective mother countries. The plantations may have been proto-capitalistic in set-up, but trade was conducted along fifteenth-century lines.

Under the "mercantile" system, a country's wealth was judged by its positive balance of external trade. The sugar islands were factories producing a commodity that would be finished in the mother country. They were also wholly and legally dependent on the mother country for all imports, and the money made in rum and sugar helped to build the foundations for British industrial society.

Left: Bar tops and booze... rum soon became respectable.

There was, however, a huge fundamental difference between a sugar island such as Jamaica and the American colonies. The latter were peopled by settlers trying to establish a new society, a fact that increased tensions. The former were mono-cultures run by exploiters interested only in making money – and little, in fact, has changed.

By the middle of the eighteenth century, Jamaica was the largest sugar producer in the world. Its plantation owners had become an important group in the British Parliament, men who could buy anything they wished with hard cash. In Jamaica and New England however, the local currency was rum, just as it was on the Guinea Coast. You couldn't produce all that sugar and rum without a huge workforce. Every spoonful of sugar, every bowl of rum punch, was made on the back of slavery.

"They took us away from our civilization,
Brought us to slave in this big plantation…"
"Declaration of Rights", by The Abyssinians (1976)

The sugar barons' logic was brutal. You needed a commodity to produce a commodity. Sugar production was labour-intensive. As plantations grew in size, so the number of slaves needed to work them increased. A large Jamaican plantation of the time generating 240 tons of sugar and 150 puncheons (a cask roughly equal to seventy gallons) of rum needed a workforce of 300. Initially, the planters used native Indians, but by 1511, African slaves and indentured white labourers were being put to work in the cane fields of Hispaniola. Criminals, revolutionaries, and religious nonconformists were sentenced to work in the Caribbean; others were "Barbadosed",

or kidnapped. Ligon felt that the indentured workers were, if anything, treated worse than the slaves – though at least at the end of their term they won their freedom.

Sugar and slavery have a long historical connection. There is evidence that the Moors used slaves, but it was the Portuguese who began trading in human flesh on a major scale. Building forts to guard their slave ports on the Guinea Coast in 1481, they held a monopoly on the trade until the start of the seventeenth century, by which time every European nation with an interest in the sugar islands was sucking Africa dry of humanity. The number of slaves increased dramatically from 1650, rising inexorably until abolition in the early nineteenth century. Over four million slaves were purchased by the sugar colonies in the eighteenth century, the bulk being sent to Brazil, and British and French territories. How were they bought? With rum.

A brutal triangle

A triangular trade was established. Britain bartered finished goods (rum, iron, etc) for flesh in Africa. The slaves were shipped to the Caribbean and sold for cash and raw materials such as molasses and rum, which would be sent to Britain. As the American colonies began to prosper, they, too, established their own triangular trade. Molasses was sent to be distilled in New England, rum was shipped to the slave coast, slaves were taken back to the Caribbean and the southern states to be sold and exchanged for molasses. America was beginning to flex its trading muscles.

Cities were built on the profits of slavery: Nantes and Bordeaux in France, Bristol and Liverpool in England, and Newport, Rhode Island in America. Most of these constructed rum distilleries to supply the slave ships. Charles Taussig's book *Rum, Romance, and Rebellion* contains the trade book of the sloop *Adventure* on its trip to Guinea in 1773. The *Adventure*, captained by Robert Champlin, left Newport loaded with local rum, which was used to barter for every requirement. Three *tuns* (large casks) of rice were the equivalent of 360 gallons; the canoe to take Champlin ashore to see the slaves held in the *barracoons* (barracks) was one gallon; six small pigs cost eight gallons. On March 22, Champlin's men began buying slaves in earnest at anything between 200 and 205 gallons for a woman, 225 for a man. When he set sail on May 1st, his cargo of sixty-three slaves had cost him (or strictly speaking, his backers) 12,632 gallons of rum. Those slaves would be sold for around £37 a head in the West Indies, and a third of the profits was immediately invested in molasses. And so the whole hideous waltz began again.

Captain Champlin lost only three slaves on the middle passage. That was unusual: the mortality rate was anything between five and thirty-four per cent. The slaving countries were debased by the trade, Africa itself was brutalized – and for what? Something to sweeten the European and American palate, to make a spirit to slake people's thirsts.

By the end of the eighteenth century, there was growing moral pressure to end slavery. As its defenders used sophistry and tortured logic to justify its continuation, an army of critics was attacking it from all angles. The philosopher Jean-Jacques Rousseau and abolitionist William Wilberforce may have argued against slavery from a moral point of view, but the argument put forth by Scottish economist Adam Smith was, if anything, more effective; mercantilism itself was coming under attack. "I believe that the work done by free men comes cheaper than that performed by slaves," he wrote in *Wealth of Nations*, a book in which he outlined a distillery as being the perfect engine of capitalism. Revolution, it seemed, was in the air.

The American rum revolution

America was built on rum. By 1640, rums from across the Caribbean were being drunk by the settlers who had brought with them a European love of spirits – and a knowledge of distillation. By 1690, rum was being produced in New England. By 1728, in excess of two million gallons of rum were being imported in addition to the molasses that was supplying the growing number of distilleries in Boston, Newport, and Medford that were selling their wares at under two shillings a gallon.

The spirit also had a more sinister side, as a way of controlling or exterminating the Native American tribes. "If your Excellency still intends to punish the Indians further for their barbarities," wrote Henry Gladwin, the English commander at Detroit, to the governor-general of Canada, "it may easily be done without expense to the Crown by permitting a free sale of rum which will destroy them more effectively than fire and sword." What rum helped start, whiskey would help finish.

Spirit of the times

Every part of American society drank – to excess by today's standards. In Virginia, planters sipped punch, flips, and toddies, (*see* page 129 for recipes); their workers downed a glass of rum on rising, then quaffed a julep of rum, water and sugar at breakfast. In the cities, work stopped for "leven o'clock bitters", while punch washed down lunch (and dinner) – after which people started their serious drinking. This was a society that knew about and enjoyed alcohol. Perhaps part of the mechanics of establishing a new society was to start brewing, distilling, and mixing; the liquids helped bind communities together. Alcohol production was symbolic: a putting down of roots. The American colonies were as steeped in rum as the cherries that were soaked in the spirit as a cure for colds.

Rum was served when preachers were ordained, during wakes, at weddings – and it was used to buy votes. The focus for this drinking was the tavern, which was also the centre of most town functions. The tavern doubled as gaol, courthouse, barracks, and hospital. Taverns were, as Peter Thompson argues in *Rum Punch and Revolution*, classless: *i.e.* democratic. They were the places where, over bowls of rum punch, a sense of American identity was forged. The first sign of this nascent "Americanness" appeared in 1733, and once again, rum was behind it.

Acts of folly

Under the mercantile system, the American colonies were supposed to be in constant economic thrall to Britain. However, the colonies had begun to trade with every island in the Caribbean, sending salt fish (itself bartered for rum in Newfoundland), timber, iron, and cotton in exchange for rum and molasses either for drinking or bartering for slaves. Much of this trade was with the French islands. Because France had banned domestic imports of rum or molasses, the islands could sell those products to the colonists at a price lower than that from the British West Indies (Barbadian molasses cost ten pence per gallon while Martinique could supply it at four pence per gallon in 1730). In 1733, despite the fact that the British islands couldn't have supplied sufficient volume anyway, the government passed the Molasses Act, which prohibited the trade between New England and non-British islands.

While the Caribbean islands had become supine sugar factories, the American colonies were organizing themselves into an independent trading enterprise, with rum as the main currency. The Molasses Act failed; there was no appreciable drop in the volumes of rum being imported and distilled, and hardly any tax was paid on it. This was the first act of mass civil disobedience by the American colonies against the mother country.

Anger intensified when a Sugar Act was imposed in 1763, this time policed by British troops and Navy. Rum was the spark that lit the revolutionary fuse. In 1776, Britain lost its American colonies and mercantilism was dead. Even that rather chilly founding father John Adams admitted that, "I know not why we should blush to confess that molasses was an essential ingredient in American independence." Yet the excessive drinking that had helped forge this sense of national identity was stoking up other problems which in 1919 would result in the Eighteenth Amendment to the very constitution rum helped to create.

By the mid-1800s, the end was in sight for the French and British stranglehold on sugar and slavery. During the 1860s, Jamaica had lost its position as the Caribbean's main sugar island to St Domingue (now Haiti), the western part of the island of Hispaniola where production doubled in the 1780s alone. St Dominguan sugar, of higher quality and half the price of that from the British islands, soon dominated the European market. Its molasses and rum went to America. However, the colony was a volatile mix of interests: rich planters, a growing (free) mulatto population, an increasing number of slaves (40,000 a year were being imported in the latter part of the century), and a paranoid and mistrustful white middle class. Each of which had its own army. When the mulatto population was refused voting rights after the start of the French Revolution in 1789, the colony ripped itself apart.

The end of slavery

In Britain, a campaign to abolish slavery had begun, driven as much by economics as morality. Prime Minister William Pitt agreed with Adam Smith that, while sugar was an important earner, the slave plantation and mercantilism were uneconomic. The future lay in free trade, and Pitt became an abolitionist – for a while. When, in 1792, the mulattos were granted the vote, St Domingue's planters turned to Britain for assistance. Help re-establish order, they told the British government, and they would agree to become a British dominion – but only with slavery intact.

Pitt changed sides. In 1794, when the radical French Assembly abolished slavery he sent troops to fight the slave army, led by the remarkable Pierre-Dominique Toussaint l'Ouverture. The British Army didn't stand a chance. Neither, however, did Toussaint l'Ouverture. In 1801, Napoleon reintroduced slavery and invaded the island, capturing the charismatic leader who died in 1803, the same year his army defeated the French. On January 1, 1804, the free republic of Haiti was born.

Haiti represented the beginning of the end for slavery. Britain abolished it at home in 1807, and in its colonies in 1833, France in 1817 and 1848. The immediate result was that sugar and rum

Right: Modern rums sold today first came to life in the ninteenth century.

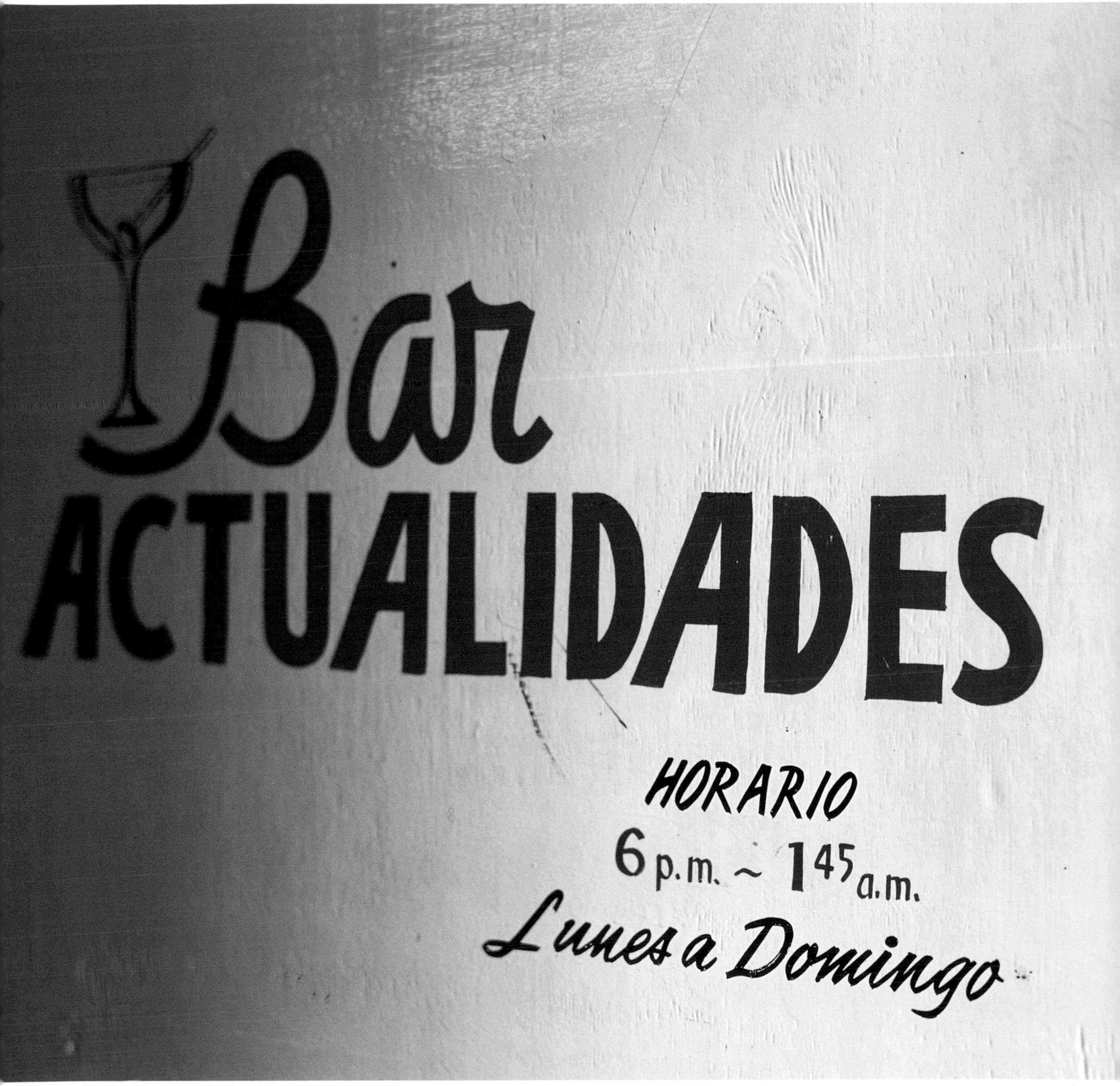
Bar
ACTUALIDADES
HORARIO
6 p.m. ~ 1 45 a.m.
Lunes a Domingo

production in French, and some British, colonies fell. Not only was sugar now being imported from India and Java, but Napoleon had turned his back on Haiti and was starting to investigate making sugar from sugar beets. By 1839, there were 457 factories in France producing thirty-two million kilograms (70.4 million pounds) of sugar a year.

As for Haiti if Toussaint l'Ouverture had not been captured, who knows? The reality was that the republic slipped back into subsistence farming while the world looked elsewhere for its sugar, rum, and molasses: to the up-and-coming colony of Guyana and to Spanish islands where slavery wouldn't be abolished until the late 1800s. It was Cuba's, and eventually Puerto Rico's, turn.

America's sugar empire

Europe may have begun to turn its back on the Caribbean sugar islands, but America was developing an insatiable sugar habit. Cuba, the largest island in the Caribbean, finally had its chance to supply this addiction, as did the unexploited Puerto Rico. By this time, sugar manufacturers had realized that the only way to produce large volumes of low-cost sugar was to create large plantations aligned to *centrales,* or centralized processing factories, and to control everything from cultivation to distribution. New technology was introduced, which made Cuban sugar the most mechanized industry in the world.

In Jamaica, meanwhile, the realization dawned that rum, for which the island was by now renowned, could generate greater earnings than sugar. Demand for the spirit in Britain was still high, and rum merchants were beginning to create their own brands. George Morton in Montrose created his Old Vatted Demerara (OVD). Lemon Hart was doing the same in London with Jamaican rums. The increase in rum production generated by the Cuban sugar boom also appears to have stimulated a new era of experimentation with style and flavour. Until the nineteenth century, rum-makers had tended to distil in a non-scientific, almost intuitive fashion. Islands developed their own styles because the planters

themselves interacted, discussing and sharing information. Now science began to play a greater part in the spirit's development.

Distillation refined

Distillers around the world had been trying to build a "continuous" still that would produce high volumes of low-cost spirit. In 1831, an Irish excise officer, Aeneas Coffey, patented a continuous still design that is still in use today. This type of still not only made more spirit, but it made a lighter one as well. Continuous-still designs popped up across Europe and were exported to the Caribbean. A lighter rum was finally achievable, which suited Cuban distillers in particular.

Distillation was hardly new on the island, but even at the start of the nineteenth century, Cuban rum-makers were admitting that they lagged behind Jamaica in terms of quality. With sugar exports growing, more spirit was being produced. There was a clear incentive to start exporting rum – but only if quality improved. Technology was the answer. There is evidence that continuous stills appeared in Cuba as early as 1848, and with them came a desire not to ape the Jamaican and Demerara styles but to make something different: a lighter rum.

Modern distilleries appeared in Havana, Cardenas, Matanzas, and Santiago, and the Royal Spanish Development Board offered a prize for ideas towards making this new rum. This caught the attention of a Spanish emigrant, Don Facunado Bacardi. In 1862, he bought a distillery in Santiago and created a revolutionary new style of rum. How did he do it? He was known to have been inspired by rums from Martinique; his still helped, as did filtration. Maybe it simply came down to paying great attention to detail.

Whatever the case, dry, light, Cuban rum had arrived. Other brands followed: Matusalem, Camps, and, in 1878, Havana Club. The world's rums could now be divided into four broad styles: Jamaican, French, Demerara, and Cuban. Although one "light" brand did appear in Jamaica, and a more delicate style began to be introduced, that island's most notable rums remained the fullest-flavoured.

Left: The mojito cocktail kick-started the first Cuban rum revolution.

The most archetypal Jamaican rum was a style known as Wedderburn, probably taking its name from the family who had extensive holdings on the island, centred around the Blue Castle plantation. Though there were still too many distilleries (148 in all) and consolidation continued throughout the twentieth century, the pungent Jamaican style was preserved. Jamaicans are hard-headed people. They weren't going to change.

Of course, the popularity of the highly aromatic Jamaican style didn't please other distillers. In Guyana, rum-makers despaired that their own technological breakthroughs weren't being given the recognition they thought they deserved. "Although the planters [of Demerara] have tried to find out the art and science of manufacturing rum ... Jamaican rum is more esteemed, merely owing to the external scent which was caused by distilling an acetous, fermented wash which had been set with rotten lees. Demerara rum is, by analysis, more perfect than rum manufactured in any part of the West Indies," wrote planter/distiller John Burrowes in 1879. That said, by that time, Guyana's distillers were supplying the bulk of the British Royal Navy's needs. Their reputation was rising.

The rums might have been improving, but in the UK, fashions were changing. Blended Scotch and Irish whiskies were the hot, new, middle-class drinks. Rum began to move downmarket, but at least it was legal. In 1919, America went dry.

Prohibition and rum-running

American distillers and saloon bar owners should have seen it coming. Though there had been Puritanical teetotallers from the moment the country was colonized, the temperance movement as we know it started back in the late eighteenth century, with "demon rum" as the main enemy. By 1833, it had one million members, and in 1851, the state of Maine temporarily went dry.

Even the direct action espoused by the Women's Crusade in the 1870s seemed to have been brushed away by the distillers. Yet this Taliban of temperance made up of axe-wielding fanatics who smashed taverns (and men's heads) would

ultimately win the day. Midwestern Protestant fundamentalism was in the ascendancy and on January 29, 1919, the Eighteenth Amendment was passed. One year later, the sale, manufacture, and distribution of alcohol was banned. Strangely, however, rum distilleries in America were allowed to continue production, the official reason being that it was needed to flavour tobacco!

Yet even with the seeming victory of the temperance advocates, America wasn't saved from the evils of drink. In fact, it started on a thirteen-year binge. Alcohol was driven underground and into the arms of a new American business enterprise: organized crime. By the mid-1920s, there were more places to buy booze in New York than there had been prior to Prohibition, ranging from swanky establishments selling the finest bootleg spirits to backstreet clip joints pushing wood alcohol to bums and deluded out-of-town hicks looking for a quick thrill.

During Prohibition, citizens knocked back liquor that had been shipped in by "rum-runners", who picked up cased goods from the West Indies and shipped them to "Rum Row", a watery boundary line situated twelve miles off the US coast and thus out of its jurisdiction. Here, the rum-runners weighed anchor and waited for the bootleggers' boats.

Despite its connotations, the moniker wasn't strictly accurate. Rum-runners like Captain Bill McCoy didn't actually ship solely rum; Whisky (Scotch and Canadian) were the main liquors. Yet rum *was* being drunk – in Cuba – and one brand in particular.

Prohibition was the start of the Bacardi phenomenon as well as the beginning of a golden age of rum cocktails. The rhythmic rumba rattle of shakers was heard across Havana, and a school of bartending emerged as Cubano, American, and European barkeeps flocked to the boom city and cross-fertilized their ideas, naming their drinks after famous customers such as Caruso, Dorothy Gish, and Mary Pickford. The cocktail craze also caught on in Europe, though recipe books of the time suggest that, while Bacardi was being drunk, most people still preferred gin in their cocktails.

Left: Remnants of Cuba's "glorious past".

If Britain's smart set was ambivalent regarding
the attractions of light rum, France made up for it
by drinking an increasing amount. The effects of
the devastating phylloxera vine louse on the wine
industry in the 1870s had forced the country to
drink rum rather than brandy, and the flavour was
a hit. By 1920, so much rum was coming into
France that the country's brandy producers
lobbied successfully for a quota to be imposed.
Once again, the colonies were put in their place.

Fall and rise

The Great Depression of the 1930s hit Caribbean
sugar production hard, and as sales declined,
distilleries closed. In 1932, a group of Antiguan
rum shop owners banded together and bought a
distillery in order to preserve their trade. In 1902,
Jamaica had a hundred distilleries; by 1938, there

were just twenty-nine. To counter overproduction,
a Rum Regulation Law was passed to cap
manufacture, and an alliance of distillers operated
a Pool Agreement to control sales and price by
means of designated "primary buyers". The era of
the big brand and centralized distillery was about
to dawn.

With whisky and gin (often of dubious
authenticity) dominating the American booze
market in the Prohibition years, rum had to wait
until World War II before it became popular once
more. Even then, it was by default. Supplies of
blended Scotch were infrequent; American
distilleries had stopped producing spirit for
drinking and were making industrial alcohol for
the war effort. The US market turned to rum – and
that meant the increasing volumes coming from
Puerto Rico, which by then had its very own

Bacardi plant, built to take advantage of the tax breaks given to the island's rums. Rum was also flowing in from Guyana and Jamaica, while Trinidad was finally getting recognition for its lighter style, thanks to American servicemen who discovered the drink while they were stationed on the island's military base.

The light brigade

Things were less beneficial for rum immediately after the war, when America's tastes changed radically. Heavy, sweet drinks were out, complicated cocktails became *passé*. In came lighter blended Scotch and a new, almost flavourless spirit called vodka. Puerto Rican rum sales fell dramatically and were only rescued by the island's innovative solution of establishing a Rum Pilot Plant to investigate the science of rum-making (*see* page 77). The new style, tax breaks, and PR campaign helped sales boom in the USA – to the detriment of rums from almost every other island. One brand was at the forefront of this success: Bacardi. By now, the brand was no longer Cuban; it was international, globalized. It had first-player advantage.

The era of the big brand had arrived. Quick to seize on this shift was Canadian whisky distiller Seagram, which began buying distilleries such as Long Pond in Jamaica, and setting up joint ventures to secure supplies for the Captain Morgan rum brand, which it launched in 1945. By the 1960s, Seagram had a presence in Puerto Rico, Mexico, Venezuela, Brazil, and Hawaii.

Captain Morgan rum was launched in Britain in the 1950's, in competition with Lamb's, a Demerara style produced by United Rum Merchants (U.R.M.), which was an amalgamation of old rum brokers and the giant sugar firm, Booker McConnell. The firm's brands also included Lemon Hart, Black Heart, and Red Heart; the last a higher-ester blend (*see* page 43) made for the South African market.

Production continued to be consolidated, except in Martinique, where fifty distillers still operated until the 1960s. It would be wrong to think that this consolidation always resulted in one plant producing huge volumes of one style of rum.

While this did happen in some cases, blenders in the UK and Europe needed a range of different rums – not just from different islands but different styles from those islands – in order to produce their brands. Were it not for those blends, the diversity of rums we enjoy today wouldn't exist.

That said, the brand-owners had no interest in talking about individual components. Drinkers in the 1930s would have known the difference between a Jamaican, a Cuban, and a Demerara rum, but by the 1960s, all that mattered was the brand. Each major island supplied bulk rums to European blenders and a selection of rums purely for local brands; Wray & Nephew and Angostura are good examples of this.

In 1959, Fidel Castro toppled the corrupt Batista regime in Cuba, and in 1961, he nationalized sugar production and distilling, effectively ejecting Bacardi from the island. The loss of Bacardi's Cuban plant may have sown the seeds of a bitter feud, but it hardly affected the brand's push towards global domination. As the 1960s progressed, younger drinkers were turning increasingly to clear, light spirits. Soon, the brand stopped being a rum; it became Bacardi.

Brand identity

Bacardi is the only drinks brand to have transcended its category. Most people don't ask for a rum and Coke, but a Bacardi and Coke. It has become ubiquitous, the spirit equivalent of Nike, McDonald's or Disney. The result has been the creation of a two-tier market. There's Bacardi and then there is "rum". But what *is* rum? It might be the best-selling spirit in the world, but its identity remains vague, its self-confidence remarkably low.

Rum's recent history has been centred on how to forge a new, premium identity and, finally, break free of its colonial shackles. From the word go, the rum industry, like sugar, has been focused on producing a cheap raw material for the outside world. Distillers are now saying "enough".

That was far from their minds in the 1960s and '70s, when UK rum sales boomed, peaking at 3.8 million gallons in 1979 – a pattern of growth that was mirrored in North America and which was triggered by an upsurge in sales of white rum, in particular Bacardi. In the UK, Bacardi was fighting against the traditional style: a dark, heavily caramelized blend of Demerara and Jamaican rums typified by Lamb's, Captain Morgan, Black Heart, and OVD. Dark rum held its own until the 1980s, but while sales were healthy, image-wise, rum remained in the doldrums.

It had never regained the middle-class popularity shed at the beginning of the century. It was a downmarket, working-class drink built on bulk shipments from across the Caribbean. Brand-owners thought that the boom would never end. But it did. The forecasts were ludicrously high, and when in the early 1970s, duty was hiked on the back of the oil crisis, Britain suddenly found itself with a rum glut. The situation was exacerbated by the fact that a new generation of drinkers were turning their backs on old-fashioned spirits such as gin, Scotch, Cognac, and dark rum. By the start of the 1980s, rum, with the exception of Bacardi, was in a slump.

Some distillers, such as Mount Gay and Wray & Nephew, had realized that the only way to survive and be profitable was to build their own brands. They were the exception. The Caribbean was still in economic thrall to the metropolis. Distillers didn't control their own destinies; bulk still ruled.

From the moment rum first appeared on the world market, it has been ring-fenced by a succession of quotas and projectionist measures. By the 1990s, the US market was dominated by "domestic" rums from Puerto Rico and St Croix, while the EU operated a duty-free quota system under the Lomé Convention protecting the rum (and sugar) industries of the Caribbean. It was clear that this state of affairs could no longer exist in a globalized economy. Strains were showing. Colombian producers had been blocked by those in Puerto Rico and St Croix over an attempt to include rum in a list of products granted privileged entry into the USA, as a thank-you in the war against drugs. Mexico claimed that, under the

Left: The luxurious interior of Bacardi's old Havana H.Q.

North American Free Trade Agreement (N.A.F.T.A.), it, too, should be able to sell its rums at the same rate as those from America's Caribbean colonies. In Europe, the French government had capped the quota on "dark" (*i.e.* aged) Caribbean rums in order to protect its territorial rums.

The system did, however, keep many rum producers afloat. They knew that, should it be abolished, then major producers like Brazil could easily undercut their bulk prices – which is precisely what has happened. The Lomé Convention has been scrapped and a "free" market created, although the EU has offered seventy million euros to the rum industry via grants to assist distillers in all aspects of production and marketing; money has been set aside for the creation of a Caribbean rum marque as well.

Post-colonial rum's dilemma

Today's rum distillers have a tough choice to make. They can keep supplying rum in bulk and slug it out for ever-decreasing margins with the Brazilians, or start bottling their own rums and sell them, internationally, as brands. One reason Bacardi has become a global player is because the firm realized the future of international brands. Bacardi also had the light rum market to itself. That is until 1993, when French drinks giant Pernod-Ricard signed a joint venture with the Cuban government to market Havana Club. Although the Bacardi staff hung a banner saying *Gracias, Fidel!* across the façade of their H.Q. when the revolutionaries rolled into Havana in 1959, the company soon became Cuba's most implacable enemy. Havana Club's sales might have been tiny compared to Bacardi's but it was a hot brand – for a time the fastest-growing in the world.

Not only had Bacardi a potential rival with international distribution, but the rival was Cuban. Like every other superbrand, Bacardi might pay lip service to free trade and the joys of competition, but in reality, it wants a monopolistic stranglehold on the market. The "rum war" between it and Havana Club was a sordid, undignified battle. Bacardi even launched

a brand called "Havana Club" in the USA, despite the fact that it didn't own the trademark. The US government then changed the law, effectively permitting it to happen. The EU responded by taking the USA to court at the World Trade Organization and won – though you get the feeling that the war is far from over.

The upside is that, faced with Havana Club, Bacardi began to market itself as a rum once more. It released a flavoured rum (Limón) and aged products. Also, stretching credibility ever so slightly, it became "Cuban". Havana Club is just one of a number of Caribbean-owned international rum brands that have emerged. The year before the joint venture was signed, Yesu Persaud, the charismatic head of Demerara Distillers Limited (D.D.L.) made a momentous decision. Realizing that there was no future in bulk production post-Lomé, he launched El Dorado 15-year-old. "I wanted to prove that we could make a drink as good as Cognac or Scotch," he said. "We have to be in brands in order to survive, and to grow, you also need a product with distinction."

A similar story can be found in Trinidad, where Angostura has woken up, smelled the coffee (with bitters added) and seen that there is no future in bulk. Its parent, CL Financial, now owns a controlling stake in Todhunter/Cruzan, a piece of St Lucia Distillers, a distillery in Surinam, Scotch distiller Burn-Stewart, and Hine Cognac. Once a Bacardi-owned subsidiary, it is now a young, go-ahead, aggressive player with its own range of international brands.

So much has changed since the first kill-devil trickled out of a pot still, but so little besides. The old colonial rum culture resulted in producers not having the confidence to sell their product to the world as the great drink it is. If rum is to achieve its potential, it must stop being a commodity and start being a brand. The twenty-first century should be the one in which rum finally divests itself of its colonial trappings and stands proud. Why? Because it is a remarkable spirit with a diversity no other can match.

It is rum's time.

How Rum is Made

Rum-making is a living process, linking nature with human sweat and ingenuity: a melding of technology and artistry. Each producer has developed its own signature style through an amalgam of chance, technology, personal preference, and pure commerce. Though every distillery is taking a sugar solution, adding yeast, and then distilling the resulting alcohol, the variables within the process are almost infinite. Cane juice or molasses? Your own yeast or a proprietary brand? How long will the fermentation be? How strong is the wash? Then, what type of still do you use: a pot or a column/continuous? Does the pot have retorts? If so, what are they filled with? If it's a column set-up, how many: one, two, three or more? At what strength is the spirit collected? Do you filter? Is it to be aged? If so, what type of oak does the rum go into, and how many times has the barrel previously been filled? How long should the rum stay in oak? A lot of decisions need to be made before you even get to how the final blend is put together. This is how rum-makers go about it.

Cane

It all starts with sugar cane. Although cane – and consequently rum – isn't like grapes (and consequently, wine) in terms of synthesizing the character of the place in which it has been grown, the soil type and climate will have an effect on the sugar levels within the cane. If you taste a range of vintage *rhum agricole* (*see* page 50) from Martinique, then you can begin to pick up the subtle differences between years. That said, where the cane is grown has only a tiny influence on the final product; fermentation, distillation, maturation, and blending all have significantly more impact. Remember: with a few exceptions, sugar cane isn't being grown for rum, but for sugar.

Which of the many varieties of cane to plant is determined by a number of factors, the most important of which is what levels of sucrose it will yield. The soil will also play a part in this decision; some canes will be better suited to clay soils, others may be ideal for bauxitic. If the sugar cane is going to be mechanically harvested, then a self-trashing variety (where the cane automatically sheds its dead leaves) may be chosen. Most cane farmers will hedge their bets and plant a selection of varieties to avoid the risk of the whole crop being wiped out by disease.

Most of the Caribbean islands will start to crop sugar cane in February and finish in June or July, although sub-tropical climates in South America allow for two crops per year. Samples are first taken from the field that is to be cut, and if the sucrose levels are sufficiently high (and the field is to be hand-cut), the field will be set on fire in order to clear the trash. Then the cane-cutters get to work, their machetes first chopping the cane as low to the ground as possible, as this is where the highest concentration of sucrose is, then lopping off the leafy tops. It is hard, hot, relentless work, but on average each person will cut three tons a day, while many will manage even more.

Speed is of the essence – as the Jamaicans say, "from kill to mill in twenty-four", because once cut, the sucrose levels in the cane begin to fall and bacterial infection sets in. The advantage of mechanical harvesting is that harvesting can run twenty-four/seven, and the cane can get to the mill quicker.

Sugar production

The sugar mill will chop, crush, and mill the sugar cane to extract its juice. This is then boiled into a syrup containing about thirty per cent sugar. After clarification, some crystallized sugar is added and the syrup is boiled again – this time under a vacuum. Sugar crystals begin to grow and, after being cooled, they are removed by centrifuge. The process is repeated twice more until all the sugar that can be crystallized has been extracted. What's left

is a thick, sticky, black-brown goo known as molasses.

Now the rum-maker can get to work. These days, most distillers use molasses imported from Brazil, Venezuela or Guiana. Even sugar-producing islands such as Jamaica or Barbados import molasses, due to the sad state of their sugar industries. Ideally, distillers want molasses with a minimum of fifty-two per cent sugars. Sadly, for rum producers, the sugar industry has become more efficient at extracting its product, with the result that the sugar levels in molasses are falling; this, in turn, can reduce the amount of alcohol obtained from each ton. On average, 11.5 tons of molasses will yield one gallon of rum at fifty-seven per cent alcohol by volume (ABV).

Once at the distillery, the pH levels of the molasses are checked and, if necessary, adjusted in order to get the most suitable level for the yeast: around 4.4 to 4.6. Because no yeast could survive in such a dense concentration of sugars, the molasses is diluted with water. The level of dilution is also dependent on which "mark", or style (see page 82), of rum is being made. In Jamaica, for example, Wray & Nephew will vary the dilution levels to help produce specific flavour compounds. Because molasses contains high levels of ash and other unwanted compounds which can hinder fermentation and cause scaling on the still, distillers will try to clarify it by a number of techniques.

Yeast

When yeast is added to the diluted molasses, the job of building flavour really begins. Yeast is a living organism which gobbles up sugars, converting them to alcohol as well as producing carbon dioxide (CO_2) and heat. For the majority of rum distillers, yeast occupies an almost mystical position in the whole distillation process. In the old days, distillers would have relied on wild yeasts, a process that is still used in the Virgin Islands by Callwood Estate (see page 81). Today, however, the majority have cultivated their own strains which they feel

produce the desired specific flavour compounds. Ask Bacardi about its rum-making process, and it is the importance of the firm's own cultured yeast that will be discussed most.

Some firms, however, have no truck with this belief in magical yeasts and use pre-packaged yeast from a yeast manufacturer. St Croix's Cruzan is one, Barbados' Foursquare another. That said, although they may think that the "magical yeast" card is a tad overplayed, all these producers have conducted extensive trials to select the specific strain – wild or otherwise – that gives them the desired end result. This is why, when other firms such as Mount Gay and West Indies Rum Distillery (WIRD) have switched from cultured to manufacturer's yeasts they did so only after ensuring that the new yeast produced a result identical to their old, cultured strain. Distillers, quite rightly, are naturally cautious people.

And what of these flavour compounds? As Mount Gay's master blender, Jerry Edwards, explains, "Yeast doesn't just produce ethanol but other alcohols such as propanol, bentonol, etc. Then there are the alcohols with higher molecular weight which boil at a higher temperature (fusel oils), which we don't necessarily want a lot of in the final product, as well as methanol, which we don't want at all!"

In addition, yeast also precipitates chemical reactions in the wash (the alcoholic liquid that is produced at the end of fermentation) which produce aldehydes, esters, acids, and other compounds that are known as congeners. These are the flavour compounds within the spirit, and each distiller will use its yeast, fermentation regime, and method of distillation to either retain or remove them.

Fermentation

It is not just the strain of yeast that helps produce these flavour compounds, but also the nature and length of the ferment: the action of the yeasts on the sugars. "The aroma

Left: Hand-cutting cane is definitely a job better left to the experts.

is born here," says Havana Club's master blender, Juan Carlos González Delgado. "The length of the ferment will affect the concentration of acids and aldehydes (esters). The longer the ferment, the higher the acidity and concentration in the aroma – which itself is a balance of hundreds of substances, all of which influence the other."

In Jamaica, Appleton's master distiller, Alty McKenzie, is of a similar opinion. "Fermentation is where you make the rum," he says. He should know; his firm takes it to greater lengths than any other.

While most rum distilleries run to a standardized fermentation time, Wray & Nephew uses different ferments as the base of its wide range of marks from pot and column stills. They can be as short as thirty hours, but equally could run for seventy-two hours or longer. Brix levels – the level of fermentable sugars in the mix – may vary; a form of semi-continuous fermentation could be utilized, and dunder could be used. Dunder is the acidic spent lees (the nonalcoholic residue left in the still after distillation) which has been aged outside in dunder pits (aka mock pits) to concentrate the acetic/butyric acids and the ester content (*see* high-ester rums, page 43).

In Jamaica, each type of rum is defined according to the concentration of esters it contains – esters being organic volatile or acetic compounds that are produced during the fermentation process. "Common Cleans" contains from eighty to 150 esters; "Plummers" generally around 150 to 200; "Wedderburns" 200-plus, and "Continental Flavoured" 500 up

to 1,700. The difference between the styles is directly linked to the nature of the ferment. A Plummer might have a two-day fermentation, while a Wedderburn will be run for longer to increase its acidity. Continentals usually have five to ten days' fermentation with dunder and cane waste added during the process.

Each distiller will run its fermentation to suit its own particular needs. A light, column-still rum is usually made from a short fermentation (twenty-four to twenty-six hours). Heavy pot-stills, by and large, come from longer ones, though Demerara Distillers (D.D.L.) uses the same wash for all its various stills. Cruzan, which makes a single extra-light marli (see page 82), runs a short, fast, and therefore potentially "hot" ferment, meaning that the vats must be cooled so that the temperatures don't exceed the tolerance of the yeast. Constant monitoring is therefore a necessity.

Controlling heat

Put simply, heat is a problem. The Caribbean is a warm place. Fermenting a highly sugary solution at relatively high ambient temperatures, often in open fermenters, can not only make the fermentation process move too quickly (leading to spoilage), but should the yeast be exhausted too soon, it can result in a weak wash. There are ways around this. D.D.L. and W.I.R.D., for example, cool the fermenting molasses by continually circulating it through a heat exchanger. "The problem with batch ferment is that you subject the yeast to a huge amount of sugar at one time," explains Jo-anne Pooler, commercial manager at W.I.R.D. "It behaves like a kid in a candy store; eating it all at once and being sick."

The answer, utilized by a number of firms (and now installed by W.I.R.D.) is to run a semi-continuous fermentation, a route taken by Foursquare's Richard Seale. He uses a closed, cooled fermenter which runs at 30°C (86°F) giving him a higher degree of control over the ferment. The molasses/water mix is drip-fed into the fermenter over a period of around seventeen hours, thereby giving the yeast a more controlled exposure to the sugars. The entire fermentation then takes about thirty-six to forty hours and results in a wash of between nine and ten per cent ABV, rather than the six or seven per cent of a shorter ferment. "It slows up the whole production process," Seale admits, "but gives us a consistent wash. As the cognac guys say, 'You cannot make a good brandy without good wine'." Appleton's Alty McKenzie would agree.

Distillation

At this stage in the production process, the rum distiller now has a mildly alcoholic, sugary liquid: a wash, not a rum. An alcohol level of seven per cent means that ninety-three per cent of the wash is water. The distiller needs to remove the water and concentrate the alcohol by distillation.

The principle of distillation is simple. Because alcohol boils at a lower temperature than water – 78.3°C (165°F) as opposed to 100°C (212°F) – when it is heated, alcohol vapours are liberated from the liquid, leaving most of the water behind. These vapours can then be condensed into a spirit. The technology might seem scary, but this is a natural, organic process. Needless to say, there are a huge number of variations a distiller can play on this basic principle. If fermentation builds in a wide range of congeners, distillation is where the decision is made as to what to keep and what to discard.

Pot stills

Originally, all rums were made in pot stills: effectively, large copper kettles similar in shape to those used in the production of malt whisky. Pot-still distillation is a batch system. In its most traditional procedure, the wash is put into the still and boiled, and the resulting vapours are collected at a strength of about twenty-three per cent ABV. Because this isn't strong enough, the process is repeated. At this point, the distiller is able to separate the "heart" of the spirit (averaging seventy-two per cent ABV) from

the "high" and "low" wines which appear before and after the heart.

The wash is made up of a large number of different alcohols and other flavour compounds (those "congeners" we talked about before), each of which has a slightly different boiling point. The lightest (i.e. those with the lowest boiling point) are the first to be liberated. The most volatile are harmful, but are soon followed by delicate, fragrant-smelling ones giving off aromas of flowers, apple, and maybe a light hint of banana. As the distillation process proceeds, so progressively heavier (less volatile) congeners are released and the aroma of the new spirit moves from delicate and floral to fruity. Oily, perhaps leathery aromas then begin to appear, but these eventually become rank and unpleasant. These heavier alcohols are referred to as "fusel oils".

That's all there is to it. The distiller's skill lies in knowing which of these congeners to keep and which to remove to get his signature style. The points at which the distiller starts and stops collecting the heart of the spirit depend entirely on which of these congeners he wishes to retain. If, for example, he wants a big, heavy spirit, he will include some of the more pleasant fusel oils. If he wishes to produce a lighter mark, then he will collect more of the higher alcohols.

These "cut points" are determined entirely by the flavours that are required. A heavy-bodied Wedderburn rum, for example, not only has a high ester content but will tend to have more fusel oils. The same goes for Common Clears and Plummers. The result is a rich, slow-maturing spirit. Steve Hoyles, Allied-Domecq's master blender, recalls one such Wedderburn which was still fine after fifty years in cask.

Pot-still distillation, rum-style, follows this principle but with a number of variations, the most common of which is the use of "retorts" that cleverly allows the distiller to produce a higher-strength spirit with a single distillation. Retorts are copper vessels containing the low and high wines from the previous distillation.

Right: As the juice flows the soul of rum starts to appear.

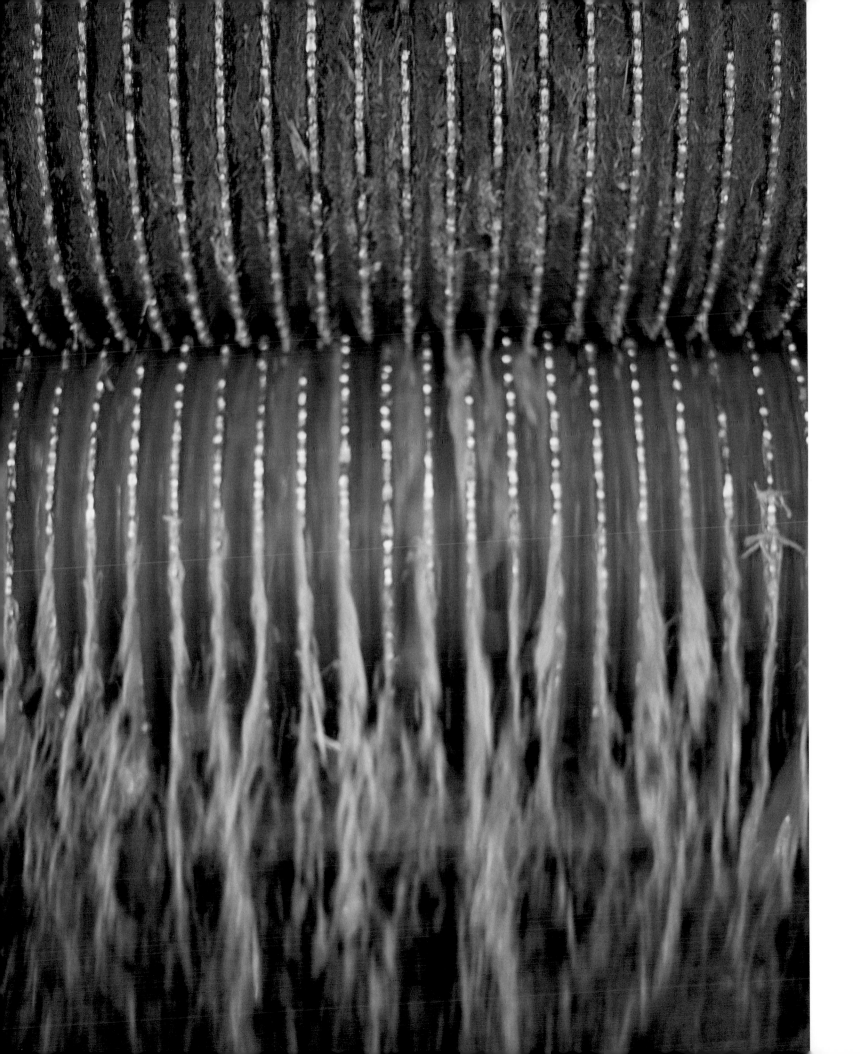

When the alcohol vapour is released from the pot, it passes into the low-wine retort, which contains an alcoholic mix (at around fifty per cent ABV) of low wines and water. Again, working on the principle that alcohol boils before water, the hot vapour causes the liquid in the retort to boil, releasing the alcohol and thereby concentrating the strength of the vapour, which is now carried into the high-wines retort. This contains a higher-strength mix of high wines and water.

The same process happens again, and the vapour, now at an even higher strength, passes into the condenser and is collected as rum. In this system, after the "heads", or beginnings of the distillate, have been separated, the heart of the spirit is collected at an average of around eighty-five per cent ABV. Once it falls below that strength, the cut is made, and the next part of the distillate (the "tails") becomes the low wine. Next, at a certain strength set by the distiller, the high wine is collected. Both are retained and used to fill the retorts for the next distillation.

The composition of the liquids in the retorts has a huge influence on the final character of the spirit. Think of the mix of liquids in each retort as being flavouring agents. By adjusting their composition, the distiller can create different results. The low-wines retort could also contain fermented wash, molasses, and dunder; there might even be some high wines! The end result, whatever the case, is a characterful, flavourful, heavy spirit which is integral to brands such as Appleton, Mount Gay, St Lucia Distillers, and the Foursquare rums.

Each distiller will use his pots in a slightly different way. Richard Seale has chilled heads on his retorts, which results in some of the vapour being condensed within the retort and falling back into the boiling liquid, a process known as "reflux". This improves the separation of the spirit into its component parts and, by increasing copper contact, makes the resulting spirit lighter.

Guyana's pot-still rums are different again: weightier but less pungent than those from Jamaica. The stills are different as well. DDL's Diamond Distillery has two types of pot still, both of which are made of green heartwood with copper necks. The single pot consists of a wooden pot, a retort, a rectifier which sits above the retort, and a condenser. The main difference (other than the wood) is this use of a rectifier: a small copper column which effectively redistils the spirit. Its function is examined more fully below (*see* The Coffey still, page 46). The resulting mark (known as VSG) is a beefy, rich spirit with notes of undergrowth, fruit, and a surprising hint of geranium.

The double pot is even more complex. Here, the copper neck of the first pot dives not into a retort but into the body of the second pot. The second pot's neck then leads to a retort, then a rectifier and condenser. Both pots are filled with wash and steam heat is applied. When they are about to boil, the steam is taken off pot number two and the vapour from number one, which comes over the neck, boils the wash in pot two. All the alcohol in the wash in the first pot is distilled to allow full recovery of all the alcohols in the second pot.

The rest of the process is the same as with the single pot. The end result is a higher level of fusel oils and a mark (called PM) which is weighty and powerful, with the aroma of black banana and overripe fruit. As ever, different flavours can also be produced by adjusting the cut points and varying the volume or makeup of the liquid in the retort.

High-ester rums

My attempts to find out about high-ester rum production in Jamaica became the stuff of high farce. No one wanted to talk about it, and once I had winkled out some of the details of the process I could see why.

Distillers, not surprisingly, want any visitor to see the best side of their plant, and high-ester rum-making is not pleasant. It *is* fascinating,

Left: In motion – cane crushing in Martinique.

however. "Think of high-ester rum as a concentrate," Main Rum Company's Ben Cross told me. He went on to explain that it was created at the Vale Royal Distillery in the early twentieth century by Jamaica's government chemist, Dr. H. Cousins, as a way of maintaining Jamaica's rum trade with Germany. The German government had slapped an *ad valorem* tax on rum in order to protect its domestic spirits industry. Dr. Cousins' solution was to produce an ultra-concentrated rum which, when added in small quantities to German-made neutral spirit, resulted in a rum-flavoured drink known as *Rumverschnitt*.

The process starts with an ultra-long ferment, which can be anything between five days and a fortnight long. Stretching a ferment in this way will result in an acidic wash containing around

500 esters. The fermenter is filled with molasses, cane juice, fruit, and, vitally, dunder which has been left to putrefy in the ground in a mock pit (*see* page 38). Made up of the acidic spent wash left at the end of distillation, the dunder contains some hugely concentrated acids, particularly butyric. "I've heard a distiller claim that he hasn't seen the bottom of his dunder pit for thirty years," says Allied-Domecq's master blender Steve Hoyles. "And I believe him."

I thought back to the sour, rotten smell that had hit me when I drove into one distillery in a vain quest to get to the bottom of this mystery. As it happened, of course, I'd been driving past the mock pits. "It's like making a good bouillon," says Carsten Vlierboom, master blender at E. & A. Scheer, "though it looks and smells horrible! Still, even if you like sausages,

would you want to go to a sausage factory?" Continental Flavoured rums are fermented in this way and then distilled in a pot still. The higher-ester examples, such as Hampden's DOK mark, start with a 500-ester rum and then re-distil it a second time to concentrate the esters still further but, crucially don't include any fusel oils. To assist this process, the distiller can fill the high-wines retort with a concentrated mixture of evaporated lime salt and sulphuric acid mixed with high/low wines and dunder. The result? Imagine a spirit that smells of nail-polish remover, glue, and decaying banana. High-ester is also made in Guyana, and at the Galion Distillery in Martinique where it is known as *rhum grand arôme*, but Jamaica remains the greatest exponent of this aromatic art.

Column stills

By the nineteenth century, when spirits consumption was rising, distillers began to search for ways in which to produce larger volumes of rum in a more efficient manner than via pot stills. In 1827, a Scottish distiller named Robert Stein made the first breakthrough. Three years later, his design was improved on and patented by the former inspector general of excise in Ireland, Aeneas Coffey. The "Coffey" (continuous) still design is still in use today; indeed, the Diamond Distillery has the world's oldest working wooden Coffey still, which is reckoned to have been producing rum for over 150 years.

Coffey's design was, frankly, ingenious. Discarding pots completely, he used two linked columns which were constructed in such a fashion so that as long as wash entered the system from one end, you would get your final spirit out of the other. Although the primary reason for inventing such a still was down to increasing volume and reducing costs, it had a secondary benefit. Because it reduced the amount of fusel oils in the final spirit and increased copper contact, a light rum could be made.

As we'll see, rum producers now utilize a number of different designs of column still to make their light and extra-light marks, but all work according to the same basic principle discovered by Stein and Coffey. Any distiller who wants to make light rum is playing games with the alcohol vapour, making it harder for the heavier alcohols to be able to be distilled.

The Coffey still

The Coffey still consists of two tall, linked columns called the analyzer and the rectifier, each of which is divided internally into compartments by a series of horizontal, perforated copper trays. The cool wash enters the rectifier in a coiled copper pipe which runs down that column and then to the top of the analyzer. Here, the wash sprays out and begins to pass down the column, compartment by compartment. At the same time, hot (live) steam is being pumped into the bottom of the analyzer. As the hot steam rises through the perforations, it meets the descending wash, and – again because of alcohol's lower boiling point – strips the alcohol from it. By the time the wash has reached the foot of the analyzer, it has had all of its alcohols and congeners removed.

The alcohol vapour/steam mix then passes from the top of the analyzer via a pipe to the foot of the rectifier and starts to rise through that column's compartments. At this point, the hot vapour meets the pipe containing the cool wash. The vapour heats up the wash, while the pipe begins to condense (reflux) the vapour. The heavier components turn into liquid and sit on each tray, while the lighter ones vapourize again and pass up the column. Think of it like *The Little Engine That Could*; those heavy alcohols want to try and get up the still, but they just can't quite do it so they fall back, exhausted, leaving their lighter cousins to go onwards.

This two-steps-foward-one-step-back progress effectively separates the lighter congeners from the more powerfully flavoured ones. The vapour eventually hits a solid plate and is drawn off into a condenser and collected,

normally at around ninety to ninety-five per cent ABV, although by positioning the plate lower in the column, a heavier rum can be made.

This is a far more effective way of separating specific flavour compounds in the spirit. Not only is reflux causing thousands of mini distillations to occur, but since the columns are tall, only the very lightest alcohols and congeners are able to reach the collecting plate (the highly volatile heads distil almost as soon they hit the rectifier and are directed back to the analyzer to be re-distilled). The column is therefore an efficient way of producing higher-strength (*i.e.* lighter-flavoured) rum.

It is light compared to pot-still rum, but all things are relative. The DFA mark which comes from Diamond's modern Coffey still has notes of banana and tropical fruit, and carries more weight than the firm's lightest marks. The EHP mark from the wooden Coffey (aka the Enmore still) is a richly flavoured spirit filled with an oily power that will give weight and substance to a blend. Bristol Spirits and Cadenhead both bottle an EHP mark. Try them if you get a chance.

Three-column stills

Almost immediately after Aeneas Coffey had patented his still, distillation entered a fertile phase of technological advancement. Light rum was now achievable, and various designs of still appeared. Bacardi's original still – a rectifying column above a pot – was just one of those. A similar design, made by Vendôme in Kentucky, has just been installed at St Lucia Distillers.

Above: Steam, sweat, the sweet smell of cane in the air at the Simon Distillery in Martinique.

Others tried to find ways to lighten the spirit even further, and by the twentieth century, three-column stills, mostly of French design, were beginning to appear. They operate on much the same principle as the Coffey still: columns divided by perforated plates, injection of live steam, etc., but with increased fine-tuning. The wash enters the top of the first column (known as the stripping column) where the most volatile alcohols (heads) can be removed.

The alcohol vapour then passes through an intermediate column, and finally to a rectifying column. Both are equipped with various ports that are positioned at specific trays from which certain alcohols (fusel oils, high wines, low wines, etc.) can be drawn off. These can either be fed back into the system for re-distillation, or they can be distilled into industrial alcohol. A distiller can make a huge range of different marks with this system. In Guyana, for example, D.D.L. makes nine different marks on its three-column stills.

Foursquare's Richard Seale also uses a three-column still, but with various modifications. For starters, he uses an energy-saving vacuum distillation in which air is sucked out of the column, reducing the boiling point of the wash to 80°C (176°F). He will use all three columns to make a light, almost neutral, spirit, but when he wishes to make a slightly heavier mark suitable for a white rum that is to be wood-aged, he will distil only in the first and last column – effectively returning to Coffey's principles! DDL and Appleton operate along similar lines. Again, the stills are being used not just to make a simple, light product but to create a range of marks giving complexity to a blend.

Multiple-column stills

Distillers are always pushing the technological envelope as far as it can go. Three-column stills still weren't efficient enough for the needs of firms making extra-light rums, such as Bacardi, Cruzan,

and St Lucia's Angostura, which wanted to remove as many of the heavier congeners as possible. All three use a multiple-column set-up.

"I was thinking of how to explain distillation," mused Guillermo Garcia-Lay at Bacardi, "and thought of Michelangelo's comment that when he sculpted a piece of marble, he simply took away everything that didn't need to be there. It's the same with making rum. You don't add anything else after you ferment the molasses; instead, you are removing components. It means that you must have the basket of components to start with – which is why yeast is so important in giving the right flavour profile. Distilling to high strength is about having the required components in a certain balance."

It is essentially a more high-tech process. In the multiple-column system, the preheated wash comes in near the top of the stripping column while live steam is fed in from the base. This strips the alcohol from the wash, giving high wines which resemble a pot-still rum in character. Cruzan then passes the vapour through an aldehyde column, which removes the heads from the high wine. Other configurations, such as that at Angostura, have a heads column sitting on top of the stripping column. The wash first passes through this set of trays, allowing the heads to be flashed off. Any heads that are collected in subsequent column can also be directed here.

At Cruzan, the vapour is then passed into the rectifying column, where unwanted alcohols can be removed, condensed, and refluxed back to the stripping column. The spirit is then condensed and collected at 94.5 per cent ABV. The two additional columns are used to process either the fusel oils or the heads, which can be refluxed into the system.

At Angostura, the spirit leaving the stripping column is condensed and passed into a column known as a hydroselector in order to remove fusel oils. This works on the principle that the heaviest congeners (i.e. those with higher boiling points) become more volatile when

Left: A classic pot/retort still at St Lucia Distillers.

The advantage of the appellation system in Martinique is that each of the island's nine distilleries operates an identical process, though each utilizes little tweaks to give its *rhum*, as the French spell it, its own particular fingerprint. The length of fermentation and the strength of the *vesou* will each have a role to play, as does the physical make-up of the still. A small, squat column will produce a heavy (low-strength) spirit; a tall one will produce a higher-strength (lighter) one. How the trays in the column are constructed also has a major part to play in encouraging reflux.

The Simon Distillery, for example, uses three different types of stills: two "Créoles", one "Savalle", and one "Barbet". The Créole still has simple, perforated plates and yields a spicy, aldehydic spirit. The Savalle operates a "chicane" system in which the *vesou*'s progress is slowed by making it zigzag down the column, thereby increasing reflux. The result is a more complex, aromatic, and floral mark. The Barbet system uses what are known as "bubble caps" (*cloches*), which sit above a chimney set in the tray. These little domes prolong the interaction between steam and liquid. Again, the result is greater reflux and a rich, vegetal spirit.

Maturation

At some stage during a tour around a rum distillery, you'll find yourself absent-mindedly caressing the smooth side of a barrel. There's something reassuring about them. Maybe it's the pregnant swell of the belly, the mysterious changes that are occurring inside: secrets that distillers are only now beginning to unlock. The more that is learned, the more extraordinary the subject of oak becomes.

The easiest way to understand what happens during the maturation process is to forget that the barrel was once part of a tree and see it as a package of flavours, all of which are shared with the rum that flows into it. Even the species of oak is important. Most rums which spend time in oak casks will be aged in once-used Bourbon

barrels made from American white oak (*Quercus alba*) which imparts a distinctive signature of vanilla, coconut, and spice. It also gives the rum its colour. Remember, every rum, no matter what style, is as clear as water when it leaves the still.

What happens during the ageing process occurs in three stages. Part of making the barrel involves charring the inside surface, a process which modifies the wood's physical and chemical composition, caramelizing sugars, increasing vanillins, and making those flavours and structure-building tannins available to the rum. If the cask wasn't charred, then pretty much nothing would happen.

Yet the char has another function. When new spirit is put into a cask, this carbonized layer removes the more aggressive edge from it as well as trapping oxygen, thereby allowing greater interaction between the air and the rum. In effect, charcoal filtration as practised by Bacardi and other producers is doing exactly the same thing, but much more quickly. By filtering and then wood-ageing all its rums, Bacardi is smoothing those rough edges off as efficiently as it can.

Throughout the ageing process, the barrel is breathing, sucking the rum ever deeper into its pores, allowing it to start extracting compounds from the oak: colour, obviously, as well as tannins, along with those evocative flavours and aromas of vanilla, coconut, spice, chocolate, coffee, orange peel, and sweet, fresh oak itself. Alcohol is also evaporating from the barrel – this is the so-called "angel's share".

As the ageing process continues, something more magical than evaporation begins to happen. Rather than the rum just taking on the characteristics from the barrel that contains it, the air, the spirit, and the wood-derived compounds begin to interact. This is where the real magic occurs, and how complex new flavours are produced. As Mount Gay's Jerry Edwards explains, "During this interactive process, those vegetal notes you get in young

Left: Recharring barrels at J.M. Distillery in Martinique.

pot-still rum are converted into fruity esters. The heavier the rum, the longer it will take for this to happen. In time, a new flavour akin to butterscotch appears."

The best way to see this process is to taste a *rhum agricole blanc* and compare it to a *vieux* (aged) spirit from the same company. It's the same spirit, but that vegetal edge has gone. Obviously, the longer the rum is left in cask, the more it will extract from the oak. It will become darker, more tannic, and "woody" until you are left with a mouthful of splinters and no rum to speak of. "The sad reality is that in hot, humid conditions, a rum of more than six to eight years old is often not pleasant, and can only be blended to produce a good result," says Tom Valdes at Cruzan. "Though we do age some rums for longer than eight years, they are used as flavouring agents in the final blend."

In addition, since Cruzan makes a light rum, the spirit is more noticeably "oaky" more quickly than in a heavy, pot-still rum. This process is driven not just by the barrel itself, but by the ambient temperature. A rum aged for five years in the cool climates of Scotland or England will be noticeably less woody than the same rum that's been ageing in the hot, humid Caribbean. Understanding and mastering "tropical ageing", as Joy Spence, Wray & Nephew's master blender, refers to it, is key to the style of her complex, aged brands. "One year of tropical ageing is the equivalent of three in Scotland," she explains. "The humidity means that the rum enters further into the oak's pores. It also means that we have high evaporation losses: six per cent a year."

This dramatic loss of volume means that firms which are ageing their rums for an extended period have to top up the barrels regularly with rums from the same batch. In addition, the more times a barrel has been used, the less it has to give the rum. Conversely, a cask which has been filled for the first time with rum (a "first-fill") will be very active with high levels of colour, flavour and tannin.

Right: "This will do!" Checking for "off" odours at Wray & Nephew distillery in Jamaica.

The second time that same cask is filled, however, the level of these active components has decreased. Eventually, you get to a stage where the cask has nothing left to give. At this point, it will either be broken down and sold on, or re-charred, which rejuvenates it. Many producers re-char their barrels, most significantly Havana Club which, thanks to the US boycott of Cuba, has had difficulty accessing fresh supplies of new American oak.

Making the grade

The fact that the flavour profile of the rum will be influenced by the number of times the cask has previously been used gives blenders a greater range of possibilities. At Mount Gay, Jerry Edwards has three grades of casks to choose from. The "A grade" (first-fill) imparts charred notes to the rum, along with vanilla, "Bourbon" notes and spices. The "B grade" (second fill) offers less, while the "C grade" (third fill) gives up less again. Each Mount Gay blend isn't just a mix of different ages of pot-still and column-still rums, but rums which have been aged in different grades of cask to different levels of maturity.

"If you just use 'A' barrels, you'll get big, rich, oaky, tannic rums which won't be enjoyable to a huge amount of people," Edwards explains. He also points out that age and maturity aren't exactly synonymous. "Age is a statement of time," he says. "Maturity is a quality which [the rum] has acquired during that time. A rum can be five years old but have the maturity of a seven-year-old, or it can be five years old and have the maturity of a two-year-old. It's like people!" When he blends, therefore, he blends according to maturity, not age.

Not every firm uses American white oak. Haiti's Barbancourt only uses Limousin oak, which has a slightly more open structure and thus allows a better exchange with oxygen as well as giving different aromatics and relatively high tannins. While at Clément in Martinique, they use a complex mix of Limousin and American oak.

Tropic of Cancer

CUBA ①

Pinar del Rio Province · HAVANA · Santa Cruz · Archipelago de Sabana · Peninsula de Zapata · Trinidad · Isla de la Juventud · Cayo Lago · Archipelago de los Jardins de la Reina · Bayamo · Pico de Turquino 1972m · Santiago de Cuba · Baracoa

Cap Haïtien · Ile de la Tortue · Parc National la Citadel · Golfe de la Gonâve · Montagnes Noires · Ile de la Gonâve · HAITI ④ · Ile-à-Vache · PORT-AU-PRINCE · Plain du Cul de Sac

CAYMAN ISLANDS ②

GRAND CAYMAN · North Sound · Queen Elizabeth II Botanic Park · LITTLE CAYMAN · CAYMAN BRAC · Brac Parrot Reserve · Batcave · GEORGETOWN · Pedro Castle ②

JAMAICA ③

Negril · Montego Bay · Ocho Rios · Dry Harbour Mountains · Blue Mountains · KINGSTON · Treasure Beach · Alligator Pond ③

PURE RUMS

Gower '03

① A Havana Club
  B Havana Club

② A Tortuga Rum (bottle)

③ A Appleton   D Monymusk
  B Long Pond   E New Yarmouth
  C Hampden

④ A Barbancourt

⑤ A Bermudez   C Barcelo
  B Bougal

⑥ A Serralles   C Fernandez
  B Bacardi   (bottle)

⑦ A Callwood

⑧ A Antigua Distillery

⑨ A Severin   E Montebello
  B Simmonet   F Bologne
  C Damoiseau G Pere Labat
  D Mon Repos H Bielle

⑩ A Shillingford C Belfast (bottler)
  B Macoucherie

⑪ A J.M.   F La Mauny
  B Saint James G Trois Rivières
  C Galion   H Dillon
  D La Favorite I Neisson
  E Simon   J Depas

⑫ A St Lucia Distilleries

⑬ A St Vincent

⑭ A Grenada Sugar Factory   C Dunfermline
  B River Antoine   D Westerhall

⑮ A Mount Gay   C Foursquare
  B West Indies Rum Distillery

⑯ A Angostura
  B Caroni

⑰ A Santa Teresa   C Licorerias Unidas
  B Pampero   D Carupano

⑱ A Diamond

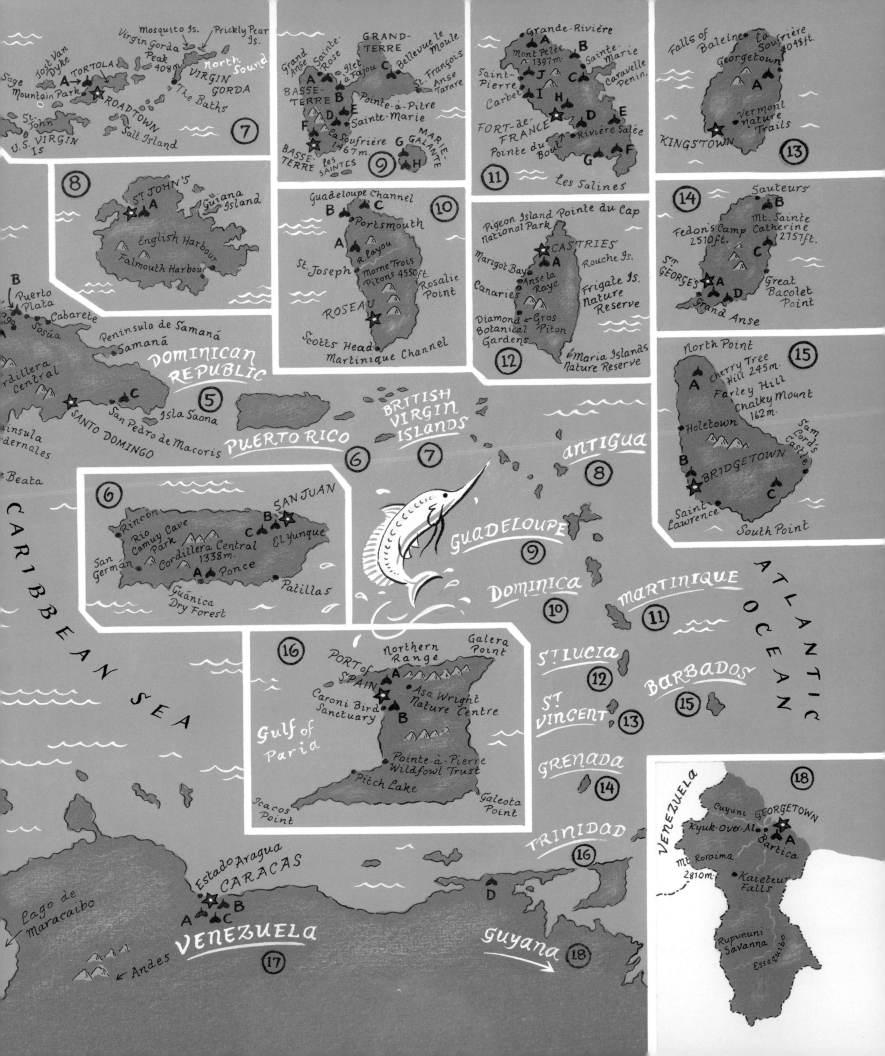

Cuba

Above: Utterly cool – that's Cuba!

Right: The realities of the US embargo are apparent.

Cuba gets under your skin and into your soul. Walk out of Havana's José Martí Airport at midnight and you are plunged into a steam bath. There are aromas of vegetation, flowers, dust, petrol fumes, sweat, and somehow, totally bizarrely, mint. Maybe it's the mouth twitching in anticipation of the first mojito...

Sadly, package tourists will never experience that first overpowering rush. The beaches of Varadero could be anywhere in the Caribbean, identikit resorts for people who want white sand, blue sky, sea – and nothing else. They don't see the lush countryside, where palm trees explode like green fireworks out of the earth. They don't meet with the people, walk the streets of Santiago, Trinidad, Cienfuego, and – most of all – the rutted, pot-holed alleys of the *barrio* of Old Havana. You know that they will never experience a little of the tough yet somehow utterly romantic life of the real Cuba. They'll never dance with total strangers at night on Havana's Malecón and drink moonshine rum that turns your chest to ice and lifts your spirits to the stars.

"At some point in their lives, every Cuban will come to the Malecón and kiss," said my friend Jorge. It's hard not to believe him. The Varadero

tourists miss all of this. They're bussed to the Floridita, where they'll sip at their frozen daiquiris and then trundle down the road on the Hemingway trail to have their mojito at El Bodeguita del Medio. Don't get me wrong; every visitor to Havana should do this. But the Varadero pack won't talk to the barmen, won't try, say, a Mary Pickford or a Mulata.

They certainly won't venture into Bar Monserrate, which remains one of my favourite drinking places in the world. Here, you get a true flavour of Havana. The house band plays at deafening volume; you find yourself sat at the bar next to hookers, musicians, cooks, hustlers, and families just having a quiet(ish) meal. Conversations start up. There's easy laughter and no hassle. Outside, the trams judder by, adding their heavy fumes to the already thick air; bicycles weave through the ruts; old cars sounding like tanks barrel along; the music pounds and sways. You become intoxicated – not with the rum (though it helps), but with the sheer force of life: the feeling that joy will somehow blot out some of the suffering.

Life here, like that in most of the Caribbean, ain't easy and it isn't made any simpler by America's economic boycott of all things Cuban. Rum, as ever, is part of this.

The cradle of cocktailization

Barbados may have been the first; Jamaica may have added its own intense spin on proceedings, while Martinique and Guyana both insinuate their own seductive charms on the drinker. But the island that first elevated rum from an interesting to a modern classic spirit was Cuba.

This largest of Caribbean islands is the cradle for most of the world's great rum-based cocktails and is home to some of the finest barmen on the planet. This is ironic, since, given its size, Cuba was relatively late on the scene as far as rum-making went. That said, by 1778, close to 50,000 gallons of *aguardiente* were being exported, rising to over one million by the turn of the nineteenth century. By 1861, there were 125 distilleries attached to the sugar plantations.

Above: Music, hustlers, new friends, and a lust for life are all here at Bar Monserrate.

Most were one-still operations, but some huge enterprises were already established (*see* page 25). There's no great surprise in this. After all, as we have seen, it was around this time that Cuba had turned itself from a minor player in the sugar market to producer of a third of the world's cane-derived sugar.

The coming of column stills

What we now know of as Cuban rum was the third broad style to emerge. In the 1860s, you could drink a range of "British", molasses-based pot-still rums from Jamaica, Guyana, and Barbados, all of which were also made in pot stills. Then Cuba, already boasting one of the most modern sugar industries, imported a new technology in the shape of the continuous, or column, still. This allowed Cuban distillers to create a new, lighter, softer, sweeter style of rum. You could call it a "Spanish" style – but I wouldn't advise it in front of a Cuban distiller.

The first (or one of the first, depending on who you believe) to perfect this light style was Don Facunado Bacardi, but whoever started things is almost immaterial. The important fact is that Cuba could now differentiate itself from the rest of the Caribbean, and while column stills soon appeared in other Caribbean islands, Cuba's light, sweet rums had stolen a march on the opposition.

This was exploited to the full during Prohibition, when Havana became a world centre of bartending creativity. That style remains firmly in place. Although the number of rums has declined since the 1930s, you can still choose from around forty different Cuban-distilled brands, all made to this light, gentle template seen at its best in the

subtle, silky, aged rums from Havana Club. The fact that the firm's rum-master, Juan-Carlos González Delgado, has managed to produce high-quality, aged spirits at a time when investment was nil and wood was hard to get hold of is testament to his great skill as a distiller and blender.

The most obvious benefit of the US boycott is that Havana is one of the few capital cities in the world to escape the effects of globalization. At a time when every other country is a carbon copy of an American model, it has retained its relaxed, scintillating individuality. No golden arches, Niketown or Gap shops here. In its bars you can find the successors to Constante Ribalagua and the other Cuban greats of the Thirties. Whether you sample the infinite variations on the daiquiri in the chilled, art deco splendour of El Floridita, the mojitos from the graffitied warren of El Bodeguita del Medio, Bar Monserrate's signature cocktail or drinks from any of the city's other great bars, you'll find bartending preserved as high art of a classical simplicity (though perhaps that's driven by necessity).

The secret of making a great aged rum – and a great mixed drink – lies in the blending. It's the same with a nation. Walk through any Cuban city, go into the markets, drink at the bars, and look at the people. Black, mulatto, Hispanic, Indian, Chinese… Cuba is a blend of people. Juan-Carlos is a great believer in how it is the combination of, and reaction between, the little components that make a great rum. It is the same with the country. It has held together since the Revolution, not because of an overly repressive government, but because of this mix, this blend of people, the tiny components in the country all sharing a similar belief in independence.

Cuba constantly throws you a curveball. One minute you're having these heavy thoughts, the next you're blowing kisses at cigar-rollers; then suddenly you're discussing global politics with someone who just wants to chat with you. Cuba scares you, seduces you, laughs at you, with you, then leaves you baffled on the side of its pot-holed streets. It insinuates itself into your system like a sweet, scintillating drug.

Very much, in fact, like rum itself.

Jamaica

There's a smell of barbecuing meat in the air; a small bottle (aka a "Q") of Appleton VX is in front of me. Jason is trying to persuade people that they want their photos taken. He has an Overproof and cranberry in front of him. The discussion between us and our new friends has turned to politics and is getting heated, yet it's still, somehow, good-humoured. The afternoon is winding gently into evening. This scene somehow encapsulates Jamaica. It is full-on yet laid-back at the same time. Circumlocution and over-polite British habits don't work here. In Jamaica, there's no fence to sit on. You leap right into the "veranda talk" and argue and laugh, rum at your side.

Having a rum close by is an integral part of the Jamaican experience. This is a country with the highest number of bars per capita in the world. Legal bars, that is. Most of the hostelries you go into have a neatly painted sign claiming, "It is my intention to apply for a licence…" When you add in the rickety rum shacks lining every road, it seems as if there could be a bar for every three people.

Rum is so fundamental to Jamaican culture that even non-drinkers will have a bottle of Wray & Nephew Overproof in the house. This is used not just as a drink, but as a medicine: rubbed on the head to ward off colds, as a cure for baldness, as an offering when any new building is being constructed. At one time, all drink was used in this semi-ritualistic way. It is also a half-forgotten link with Africa. No other country I can think of has such a close, complex, relationship with one spirit brand.

The strong, silent type

Maybe part of its success is due to its strength. "It's *real* rum," I was told on more than one occasion. The same was also said about "JB". Ask for this in one of the bars on the north coast and, after being given a suspicious look, a bottle will be produced from below the counter and a hefty shot of moonshine will be poured. JB (meaning John Crow Batty or Vulture's Arse) is either illicitly distilled rum or semi-legally acquired new-make straight from the still. It hits like lightning in the throat. "Drink it down, mon!" they laugh as you gasp for breath. The pain is worthwhile. The ice has been broken and the veranda talk starts up.

To experience this and discover Jamaica in all its in-your-face, frustrating, joyous reality, forget the hermetically sealed, all-inclusive resorts. Head into Kingston, up into the hills or down to the quiet south coast and sit with a Q of rum and some jerk pork or chicken served with mouth-searing, addictive pepper sauce and let life wash over you. It's not that difficult to escape the irritating hustling that blights the north-coast resorts. A short, if bumpy, drive will take you through a land of domed mountains, dense forest, and hidden communities. You'll drive past rum shacks, people offering ice-cold "jelly" (fresh coconut), fish-fryers, shrimp-sellers, honey-makers, and sudden, surreal sights like a rasta with a vase of plastic flowers on his head walking calmly down the road in the middle of nowhere.

Familiar names appear: Paisley, Dumfries, Perth, straggly places with crude shacks clinging to the fertile hills next to new mansions being built by returnees. It is desperately, frighteningly poor and rich at the same time. Those names speak of the days of slavery, the continued poverty, the result of a country still being bled dry by European

Above: A "soon come" mentality prevails.

Right: Relaxing, Jamaica-style, in Falmouth.

sugar firms. The fact that the biggest houses are being built by expats just underlines the fact that, to succeed, most Jamaicans have to leave the island.

At one government-owned sugar estate, a startlingly blond child runs out of the great house to see us, quickly joined by his equally blonde mother. "Welcome to the new Zimbabwe," she says, turning on her heel and walking off. Turns out the estate had been compulsorily nationalized by the government. Has she a point? I ask the locals at the next bar. "Nah, mon," comes the answer. "Dey ruin de estate. De people are sufferin'." A woman quotes Bob Marley: "Dem belly full, but WE hungry".

Trouble in the fields

It isn't as simple as that. The sugar industry is near to collapse. Underinvestment means sugar is inefficiently produced, and therefore expensive. One solution is modernization, but that will result in jobs being lost in the poorest areas of the country. Then again, if the multinational sugar companies would finally allow a sugar refinery (the profitable part of the process) to be built in Jamaica, not only would jobs be saved, but money might be reinvested. Until then, the Jamaican sugar industry remains between a rock and a hard place.

That means that most of its distilleries are in a bad way as well. If anything, it is the rum industry that has been keeping most sugar factories afloat. It happened with Innswood, though it is now, sadly, closed. It is no exaggeration to say that E. & A. Scheer, the major European bulk importer, managed to keep rum distilling (and therefore sugar production) going at Hampden, while it has been the needs of Captain Morgan that has maintained sugar and rum-making at Long Pond and Monymusk.

Not only do these factory-distilleries provide much-needed employment but, crucially for rum-lovers, their continued existence has meant that classic rums continue to be made. All three stills produce magnificent examples of all of Jamaica's classic pot-still rum styles. Should they close – which could well happen if the sugar industry does collapse – a centuries-old heritage, a part of

Jamaica's individuality, its pungent, punchy soul, would virtually disappear. It would be the equivalent of every malt distillery closing on the island of Islay.

They will only be saved through massive investment and some pretty tough decisions, something that Wray & Nephew has done at its Appleton Estate. Here, the sugar factory has been modernized, with the distillery next in line. While rum may never overtake sugar in importance, it is an increasingly important element in Jamaica's attempts to get its economy back on an even keel.

It's strange to be thinking of this while standing in the beautiful hidden valley where Appleton Estate is situated. The cane fields glow in the sun; there's a heady perfume of molasses, banana, and tropical fruits in the air. Some distilleries just seem right, somehow, emanating a feeling that a great spirit is made here. This is one of them.

The growth in exports for Appleton brands is encouraging. While sugar may never become the junior partner to rum, it's clear that it is the spirit which holds a key to Jamaica's future growth. The quiet, precise way in which Alty McKenzie and Joy Spence create and work with their rums, the manner in which Joy uses the variety of marks to create complex blends, means that the Appleton rums are among the greatest Caribbean rums of all.

Needless to say, they are quintessentially Jamaican; you wouldn't expect an anonymous, bland rum from this country. Drinking them on their own, you might not automatically notice the lift that the use of higher ester rums gives to Jamaican blends, but put them in a multi-island line-up and they leap out at you, saying, "I am Jamaican!" Strangely, I am reminded of peaty Islay malts, not in aroma but in their defiant adherence to an apparently unpopular style. The aroma may have been looked down on by other distillers in the past, but it isn't in the Jamaican character to give up. They knew they had something different, something special, something with character and individuality. Today, these traditional pot-still rums are only one among the many different styles and ages that Joy Spence crafts into the Wray & Nephew range. A complex *mélange* from a complex and wonderful country.

Right: Rum, reggae, and Rolling Stone titles: Jamaica has it all.

Today's MENU

✓ Chicken Fried ← $160 - L.
130 SM.

Curry Goat $200

Steam Fish : Done To Order

FRIED FISH 🐟

PORK { JERK ← 1b $350
       STEW ← $200

SOUP - GOAT HEAD
L $100

Special
Curry Goat   S $50
Head + Belly

Dominican Republic / Haiti

"Haiti? You gotta go, man! It's the wildest,
craziest place you'll ever visit!" My Jamaican
friend was cackling and shaking his head as
he began recounting stories which would
make even the most hardened traveller think
twice about ever catching that flight to Port-
au-Prince. Or at least, take a huge amount of
care and be armed with a well-honed sense
of humour when he arrived. It seemed only
appropriate that, when the initial hilarity
subsided, his enthusiasm about this forgotten,
impoverished country revolved around two
things: its beauty and slightly worrying
edginess. Two contradictory aspects living
side by side – which, when you think about
it, has been typical of the island of Hispaniola
since the start of the nineteenth century.

Everything is split into opposites in Haiti. It
is abjectly poor – the poorest country in the
Americas –- but its rich elite are wealthy. It is
the cradle of democracy and black nationalism
in the Caribbean, yet its people lived under
dictators until recently. It is half of an island
which was, at the end of the eighteenth century,
the powerhouse of sugar production in the region.
Today, its eastern neighbour, the Dominican

Republic, is building a tourist industry, but there are
no beach resorts and Caribbean wedding packages
being offered in Haiti. It's the place of poor
refugees, of Hollywood-style voodoo. Even its rum is
different. While the Dominican Republic makes
rums in the Cuban style, Haiti's rum is "French".

The forgotten island

Rum-drinkers tend to overlook this island. It
might be the second-largest in the Caribbean
and, in Santo Domingo, has the oldest city in
the Caribbean, but it, especially the Haitian part,
remains enigmatic.

As the Spanish colony of Hispaniola, this was
one of the first islands to grow sugar; there was a
sugar mill working here in 1516. It is pretty likely
that some sort of rum would have been made
soon after that. By the eighteenth century, the
island had been partitioned into its French-
controlled western part (called St Domingue) and
a small Spanish colony in the east.

High-quality, well-priced sugar, tobacco, indigo,
coffee, and (of course) rum flooded out of St
Domingue's plantations, making European
merchants and the plantocracy extremely wealthy.
As we have seen (*see* page 22), the Haitian
revolution was the catalyst for a reappraisal of sugar
and the Caribbean. The aims of Pierre-Dominique
Toussaint l'Ouverture came to nothing. He died, his
feet gnawed by rats, in an Alpine prison, and with
him went the idea of black liberation and equality
in the Caribbean. Haiti paid for its effrontery. The
world turned its back on the country.

Things were little better for the third independent
state in the Americas, the Dominican Republic.
Until the Americans made it part of its sugar
empire in the end of the nineteenth century, it,
like Haiti, remained a peasant economy. Like
Cuba and Puerto Rico by the 1930s, it was under
tight American fiscal control, its economy
dominated by massive sugar firms, and until the
1960s, it was run by a vicious dictator.

While Haiti remained forgotten, the Dominican
Republic was still seen as offering an opportunity
to immigrants. Men such as Armando Bermúdez,

Don Andrés Brugal Montaner, and, in the twentieth century, Julián Barceló all left Spain to make their fortunes in the Caribbean. Their families still make the rums they created. Bermúdez started using his pot still in the mountain town of Santiago in 1852. Brugal, who learned his distilling craft in Cuba, arrived in the north-coast town of Puerto Plata a few years later and began distilling there. Brugal rums are still matured in the town.

In many ways, the story of Julián Barceló mirrors that of his predecessors – with one exception. He didn't leave his homeland of Mallorca in 1929 to work in sugar; he went to make rum. The year after his arrival, a hurricane obliterated the sugar crop – but distillers are hard men. Barceló is now the most active of the Dominican Republic's rum producers internationally. Why, though, hasn't this country – which, after all, was one of the triumvirate of American "colonies" making sugar in the early twentieth century – managed to create a larger following for its rums? As ever, the roots of the answer lie with sugar.

A well-kept secret
As an independent country, the Dominican Republic didn't get the tax breaks doled out to Cuba and, more generously, to Puerto Rico at the start of the 1900s. While the latter could target the USA with its rums, and Cuba (pre-Castro) built its reputation as the rum "party island", the Dominican Republic's sugar went to Europe. Its rum? That stayed at home.

Anyone who has holidayed in the Dominican Republic will have tried and enjoyed the rums that are stylistically close to their Cuban cousins: soft, gentle, column-still spirits showing smooth elegance from (often long) maturation in American oak. Today's domestic market is dominated by Brugal (which also owns the Macorix brand), while Barceló is beginning to look further afield and has already made inroads in Spain. Bermúdez also focuses on the increasingly healthy home front.

The growing tourist industry is making all the Dominican Republic brands better known, and it's high time that the country's rums (and cigars)

were given more serious consideration. What's still surprising is how long we have had to wait.

When you study how sugar rose and fell on each of the Caribbean islands, one fact is evident: each time the sugar industry found a new home, a new style of rum was born. Each island shone briefly, but rum remained: a liquid legacy, a sweet residue in the memory. No one island could ever dominate sugar for long. Empires fell, trading conditions changed, alliances shifted, the land was exhausted. But each of the great sugar islands – Barbados, Jamaica, Puerto Rico, and Cuba – became known for making a new, unique, style of rum. The only exception was Hispaniola.

That isn't to say it doesn't make wonderful rums. Haiti may be the poorest country in the Americas, but it still, somehow, makes one of the world's greatest rums: Barbancourt. The firm was founded in 1862 by Dupré Barbancourt, who, coming from the Charente, imported cognac technology to Haiti. Even today, the firm operates a double-distillation system and ages exclusively in Limousin oak barrels. His nephew, Paul Gardère, started to distil in Port-au-Prince; Paul's son, Jean, relocated the distillery to Plain de Cul de Sac. Jean's son, Thierry, is now in charge of the firm. Made in the "French" style, Barbancourt uses *vesou* (wash) extracted from crops harvested not just from its own plantation but from 200 other growers. Thierry estimates that the distillery is indirectly responsible for 20,000 people – a reminder of how rum-making isn't just a technological activity, but a craft that affects the lives and livelihoods of entire communities.

The rum is first distilled in a column still and then finished in a pot (and collected at ninety per cent ABV) The spirit is then barrelled at very low strength (fifty per cent ABV), a technique that necessitates long maturation. The Gardère family's resilience is a triumph of the human spirit in Haiti. They don't only produce rum; they make a rum with a finesse that is almost unsurpassed in the world. That is the final, surprising contradiction of this too-easily-dismissed country.

Left: Is that straight or have I had one too many...?

73

Puerto Rico

Between them, Cuba and Puerto Rico changed the way people think about rum. They developed a new style, one in which science played as important a role as intuition: a rum that was lighter and appealed to the public's changing tastes.

Vitally, Puerto Rico made postwar America start thinking about and drinking rum once more. In a few short years, Puerto Rico moved from an exploited sugar colony to a mass-market rum producer. The story of its rum is the spirit's history in miniature: innovation and determination being influenced by politics, colonialism, globalization, and protectionism – and you can drink the evidence!

Yet the origins of Puerto Rican rum are obscure. You have to wait until the sugar boom of the nineteenth century to start unearthing evidence of spirits production here, which appears to have come in on the back of an influx of foreign sugar planters (French, British, Dutch, American, and Spanish). As they arrived on the island, they brought with them new sugar-making technology. It was the Spanish émigrés, however, who were to have the greatest impact on rum-making.

In 1865, Don Juan Serrallès imported a still from the French firm Egrot Frères, one of the great

Above: Gazing out over the lush Caribbean landscape.

Right: Liming at the hairdressers.

pioneers of still design, and installed it on the family's Hacienda Mercedita estate. By the end of the century, Pedro Fernandez's Ron Barrillito brand was being marketed, and some rum was being exported to Spain and, tentatively, to the USA. In 1897, the year before America took control of the island, Puerto Rican distillers managed to export 18,000 gallons of their rum to their nearest neighbours.

It was not a hugely confident start for what would become one of rum's most remarkable associations, and it would be many years before America began drinking Puerto Rican rum in earnest. There were brands, but this was a local product for local people, and most of the rum that was being drunk was moonshine. Puerto Rico was also a poor country where cane workers were the highest-paid employees, earning a princely thirty-five cents a day (so no fancy brands for them). It was sugar that was Puerto Rico's first major export.

The result of being a *de facto* American colony was that Puerto Rico became a vitally important component in the USA's sugar empire. In 1899, the sugar industry controlled fifteen per cent of the land available for cultivation. By 1930, it was forty-four per cent, and thanks to favourable quotas fixed by the US government, the island was producing forty per cent more sugar than Cuba.

The predominantly US-owned sugar firms were doing very nicely, and the American sugar lobby wanted it to stay that way, successfully blocking attempts by the Puerto Ricans to win full statehood and banning Serrallès from exporting its refined sugar to the USA. Just as in the days of European mercantilism, the colony was there to produce raw materials, not finished goods.

The effects of being an exploited colony were clear to see. By the 1930s, Puerto Rico had been bled dry. The island was still living the life of a grand plantation and was entirely reliant on sugar. It couldn't even make rum during Prohibition, though, given the poverty of the island and a lack of other export markets, Puerto Rican distillers still managed to do pretty well for themselves. The USA realized that a massive

Above: Sun, ships, and cane: rum's rich history.

investment programme was needed to bring Puerto Rico into the twentieth century, and it was agreed that the Treasury Department would give the Puerto Rican government an annual sum equal to the excise duty paid by the American importers of Puerto Rican rum.

Coming of age

It was a generous, farsighted tax break which meant one thing: rack up rum production and rebuild the island. From being a secondary concern behind sugar, rum suddenly found itself centre stage, and it remained there. As soon as Prohibition was abolished, Serrallès built a new distillery in Ponce. Meanwhile, as a firm with its eye on the big picture, Bacardi noted that Puerto Rican rums didn't incur any US import duties – unlike the rum the company was making in Cuba.

In 1936 a small plant had been built on the site of an old Spanish gaol in San Juan, saving Bacardi $1 a bottle on import duty.

In hindsight, Puerto Rico gave Bacardi its first step up towards global domination. The World War, if anything, helped the Puerto Rican industry. With the domestic whiskey business shut down (again) and imports of Scotch sporadic at best, the American public turned to Puerto Rican rum to soothe their war-jangled nerves. Between 1943 and 1946, 16.7 million gallons were imported.

You could be forgiven for thinking it was plain sailing from then on, but during the war, people drank anything, and the demand for rum was so high that quality plummeted. When peace was finally declared, little loyalty remained for what had been, in effect, an alcoholic security blanket. Sales collapsed.

In addition, America was beginning to go light. Vodka was starting its rise, sales of blended Scotch rather than Bourbon were growing; old-style heavy rums became unfashionable. Stylistically, something had to happen to win back the American consumer. This was achieved through a two-pronged (and very modern) attack. Consumers were wooed by PR campaigns coordinated by the Puerto Rican Rum Program (funded entirely by the tax breaks granted by the US government) and through improved quality.

Luckily, Puerto Rico was home to one of the great figures in rum-making, Rafael Arroyo, who in 1936 had embarked on the first serious scientific study of rum production. Arroyo's investigations were interrupted during World War II, but afterwards his studies became more relevant than ever and are still regarded as essential reading for rum distillers. In 1953, the *Planta Piloto de Ron* (Rum Pilot Plant) was founded, its brief to investigate every aspect of rum-making and pass on the information, free, to any distiller who wanted to use it – whether based in Puerto Rico or not. The result: the creation of the lighter-bodied style of rum that still dominates the world. Today, Puerto Rico produces thirty-five million proof gallons of rum a year, the bulk of which is exported to the USA.

By the mid-1950s, Puerto Rico had realized that distilling rather than sugar-making represented a more profitable future. By the end of the decade, sugar was dead and the rum firms were importing their molasses from the Dominican Republic. Modern rum was born out of a synthesis of PR, production, and a consumer-driven intent. Things would never quite be the same again.

In 1958, Bacardi opened its massive distillery in Catano: a clear statement of the firm's ambition. All Bacardi sold in the USA is made here, generating huge revenues for the Puerto Rican government and the rum PR campaign. Serrallès, however, is the biggest seller on the island, living evidence of the quality ethos articulated by Arroyo. Its Grand Añejo is proof that this island produces world-class rums, and that light need not mean bland.

Virgin Islands

Above: A shrine: to rum.

Right: Life can be simple in the Caribbean.

What is now the US Virgin Islands has a history that's as confusing as it is strange. Even in a part of the world where, often, islands have had more rulers than Billy Bob Thornton has had wives, the US Virgin Islands' colonial history is a web of claim, counter-claim, invasion, land grab, and purchase. Seven nations have ruled them at one time or another: Spain, England, Holland, France, Malta, Denmark, and, finally, the USA, which, seeing a prime piece of tropical real estate, bought the islands for $25 million in 1917.

Sugar production, and thereby distilling, was kicked off by the French in the early seventeenth century, but grew in importance – and volume – when British planters arrived; even when the islands were a Danish colony, most of the plantations were British-owned. Each plantation would have not only produced sugar but made its own rum to its own recipe which, contemporary sources indicate, was akin to a heavy-bodied, Jamaican pot-still style. Also, like their Jamaican cousins, these rums had a considerable reputation in the New England colonies. George Washington thought so much of the rums produced in St Croix that he supplied the island's rum to his troops at Valley Forge.

By the end of the eighteenth century, there were 114 windmills and 144 animal mills crushing sugar cane. Rum became an increasingly important part of the economy, exchanged as barter for essential goods, and sold in larger volumes when the price of sugar dropped.

St Croix rum today

The plantation economy has had its day, the St Croix sugar empire is a folk memory, the new great houses are owned by millionaires wanting a paradisiacal retreat, and the ruins of the windmills and factories on St Croix are a living archaeology. You read the stones, looking for clues in the jumble for mill and still. The island has moved on since those boom days of the late eighteenth century. And as the island has changed from a sugar-based economy to one heavily reliant on tourism, so has the art of making rum – though its importance is as great now as it was in Washington's day, thanks to the Nelthropp family, which has been distilling on St Croix for seven generations.

The days when pot stills were attached to every sugar factory are gone. Sugar cane hasn't been grown on the islands for thirty years. Yet thanks to the Nelthropp's Cruzan distillery (which, while being owned by importer Todhunter, still has heavy family involvement), rum remains central to St Croix's identity. The style may have changed – the heavy, pot-still rums have gone the way of the windmills – but the attention to detail has remained.

The Cruzan (the name means a native of St Croix) rums are light-bodied. They are made in a sophisticated, five-column still, and a complex blending regime is utilized to produce a spread of different flavours, aromas, and textures. Unlike other producers, only one style of spirit is made here; neither is a secret yeast culture involved. The key to the modern Cruzan style lies in the distillation and the blending of rums of different ages.

All of the rums are aged for a minimum of two years in steam-cleaned, ex-Bourbon barrels. With a light distillate, Cruzan steers away from giving its top rums extended wood-ageing, though the

Above: Time for a sundowner!

two-year-old will have some four-year-old blended in, and the five-year-old and single barrel both contain a small amount of twelve-year-old rum in the blend (the single barrel is a blend of different ages which is then "finished" in a new, white-oak barrel).

Why the dramatic shift in style? Like their colleagues in neighbouring Puerto Rico, the Nelthropps saw that the postwar US market – which, after all, has been the main purchaser of St Croix's rums since colonial times – was going light. Call it a consumer-driven decision, but innovation (the development of single-barrel rum for example) and attention to quality have remained paramount. Perhaps being steeped not just in rum-making but in an appreciation of its importance to St Croix's heritage has helped. Whatever the case, as premium rum expands globally, Cruzan is still flying St Croix's flag.

British Virgin Islands

The situation couldn't be more different in the British Virgin Islands (B.V.I.), a cluster of thirty islets, sixteen of which are inhabited. Here, unchanging tradition and memories of rum's naval heritage are key. Half-heartedly settled by the Spanish in their search for mineral wealth (there was a copper mine on Virgin Gorda at the start of the seventeenth century), the B.V.I. were briefly a Dutch colony in the seventeenth century, before the English took control in 1680 and continued what the Dutch had started: sugar plantations and rum distilling, primarily concentrated on the main island of Tortola.

The nineteenth-century sugar slump hit the B.V.I. hard. It wasn't until the middle of last century that the islands we now know today emerged as a yachting paradise, eco-tourist destination, and offshore banking haven.

Tortola may be the quintessential sophisticated Caribbean destination, but its sole rum distillery retains potent links with the past. The Callwood Distillery is the last of Tortola's seven distilleries, and is remarkable in a number of ways. It claims to be the oldest continuously running distillery in the eastern Caribbean, and is one of the few British distilleries making rum from sugar cane juice rather than molasses. This is living, artisanal rum-making: a process that has changed little in its 400-year history, offering a glimpse into the way the spirit was made centuries before column stills appeared and marketing departments arrived. This is rum that speaks of its past, of the personality of the people who created its original individual style. It is the polar opposite of Cruzan.

Here, the wild yeasts that live on the sugar cane are allowed to do their job in their own time, and this long fermentation undoubtedly adds its own range of flavour compounds to the finished product. The pot still is directly fired; the rum runs straight into the barrel. There are many other distilleries like this in the Caribbean, but they are hidden in the hills, out of sight of tax men and police. Callwood is on show. Its hand-bottled, hand-labelled white and three-year-old rums are essential additions to any rum-lover's cabinet.

Tortola is also where Pusser's Rum is blended and bottled. This British rum style, ironically, was saved by a Canadian. The pusser (a corruption of the word "purser") on board British ships was the man who issued the daily tot of rum (*see* page 119). When that practice was abolished on July 31, 1970, a Tot Fund was set up by the British Admiralty with the not-inconsiderable sum it would have spent on a year's supply of rum.

Pusser's Rum, however, was on the verge of extinction until ex-US marine Charles Tobias persuaded the Royal Navy to let him use the name, provided he stuck to the Pusser's recipe (said to be based on a blend of six different rums from Guyana and Trinidad) and donated a set amount from each case sold to the Tot Fund. The deal was done, the brand was saved, and another rum could call Tortola home.

Guyana

After drifting around the islands of the Caribbean, Guyana, on the east coast of South America, takes you by surprise. There are no coral beaches here, no surf: just a web of canals and the lap of the coffee-coloured rivers against the wharves. Names of settlements flash by: Supply, Relief, Canaan, and Garden of Eden, speaking of past empires, business, and religion. Hindu temples and mosques sit next to evangelical churches and roadside barber-shops. Prayer flags clack on bamboo poles. Emaciated mules haul goods to ramshackle markets. In Georgetown's wide avenues, the sound of Sunday service echoes from the huge wooden cathedral, mingling with the cricket commentary on hundreds of radios.

Guyana might be located in South America, but it thinks of itself as Caribbean, and it's as much East Indian as it is African. It is independent, but has retained the old-fashioned manners of the colonial era. Although it was the Dutch who established the territories of Essequibo, Demerara, and Berbice in 1650, rum began to be made only when English sugar planters arrived some decades later. By the eighteenth century, every

plantation was exporting rum, their wares identified by the plantation "marks" that are still used today. Albion became "AN", Port Morant "PM", Uitvlugt (pronounced "eye-flat") "ICB/U", Enmore was "EHP", and Blairmont a "B" within a diamond. By the nineteenth century, the Demerara style had become the main constituent of British navy rum and had been embraced by British blenders.

Diamonds in the dust

Like everywhere in the Caribbean, Guyanan rum's recent history has been dominated by consolidation, sugar, and politics. By 1971, the 200 distilleries that once worked here had been reduced to three: Enmore, Uitvlugt, and Diamond. Today, only Diamond, run by the privately owned Demerara Distillers (D.D.L.), continues to make rum.

Diamond is unlike any other distillery in the Caribbean. That region is littered with the echoing shells of old plants, the stills long gone, the memory of their spirits evanescent. Not here. In Guyana, men like D.D.L.'s spirits director, George Robinson, recognize the importance of tradition, flavour, and diversity. George was a first-class cricketer, an opening bat, and you can see his playing style even now. He is patient, taking things steadily, playing himself in, steadying the younger, rasher members of the team. He's not flashy, but a man who quietly builds a mammoth innings.

He stands at Diamond's stillhouse and laughs as my jaw falls to the floor. Here are single and double wooden pots, Savalle columns, Coffey stills, a high-ester still, a tiny pair of copper pots, and, on the back wall, looking like a giant filing cabinet, the Enmore still: the last working wooden Coffey still in the world, which has been producing Demerara rum since 1880. This isn't a museum; these are all working machines and have been saved, thanks partly to D.D.L., which recognized Guyana's extraordinary wealth of distilling equipment, but also by blenders who needed the diverse range of marks. Nowhere else could make "PM" (Port

Morant), so when that distillery closed, its wooden double pots went first to Uitvlugt, and then in 2000 to Diamond, when D.D.L. closed Uitvlugt. It's the same with the single-pot still, which went from Versailles to Diamond, again via Uitvlugt. Or the Enmore. Or the Savalles.

Marks of distinction

You might expect the marks to be variations on a theme, with overlapping flavours. Instead, each is distinct. There is a clear stylistic difference in them all – and there are nine from the Savalle stills alone, out of the many created here. Each provides a new glimpse into the past, of how distillers used local materials and new technology; of intuitive distilling; of improvisations which, whether by design or chance, resulted in each plantation making its own variant on the Demerara style – though few people really know what that is.

True, Demerara rums have long been obliterated by caramel, their subtle, soft, medium-bodied style not allowed to shine. At least that was the case until 1992, when D.D.L. began to break free of the chains of bulk. Company chairman Yesu Persaud had a vision. What he realized was that if his firm were to prosper, it had to do so with its own premium products. He announced this intention with the launch of El Dorado fifteen-year-old, widely regarded as the quality benchmark for aged rums. The El Dorado range now includes a superb twelve-year-old, a dangerously drinkable five-year-old, and, more recently, a standard white, gold, and dark.

D.D.L. also owns its own distribution companies in Europe, the USA, and India. Naturally, the bulk business will continue – after all D.D.L. is the only distiller which can make these marks – but Persaud's vision is to see rum taken seriously. "Our decision to go premium was to show what real rum was," he said. "We knew rum was a commodity and that it was only a matter of time when we would have to change. I wanted to be ahead of the game."

That also meant breaking free of the past. Guyana was the plantation economy writ large. It is hard to imagine your country owned by a single corporation, but by the 1960s, the British company Booker McConnell was growing eighty per cent of Guyana's sugar and made most of its rum as well, much of which was then sold through London-based United Rum Merchants, of which Booker was a founding member. Following nationalization in 1976, the (Booker-owned) Guyana Distilleries (an amalgamation of the distilleries at Skeldon, Port Morant, Blairmont, and Albion, based at Uitvlugt), the same firm's Demerara Distillers (based in Enmore), and Diamond Liquors (the rum division of sugar firm Sandbach Parker) were brought under the umbrella of a state-controlled holding company, Guyana Liquor Corporation, headed by Yesu Persaud.

The way in which Persaud managed to make the Guyanan government a minority shareholder in a company it was meant to control is a book in itself, but the end result was the creation of D.D.L. and a new force in world rum. "It was tough," he admits, speaking of the days when Guyana's economy was run on strict Marxist lines. "Everyone thought we'd be written off, but we survived."

Guyana is still poor, still saddled with enormous debts, but there is an almost serene determination about its people. Standing on the pier in the port of Parika, George Robinson and I watch an overladen ferry head across the River Essequibo towards islands the size of other Caribbean nations. I think of the other ships that left this country laden with its wealth, the ones that docked carrying slaves, indentured East Indian labourers, and white planters ready to make their fortunes on the sweet banks of Demerara.

We retire to the staff club at Uitvlugt, where a white-jacketed barman brings us drinks on the deserted terrace. As the sun goes down, we chat about cricket, sugar, and rum, the rights and wrongs of the system, of his days here, of dinner dances and camaraderie. A light breeze brings little ghosts nuzzling up to us, whispers from a happy past.

What of the future? D.D.L. is well-placed in the new world of Caribbean-owned, branded premium rums. "It is time for real rum," Yesu Persaud had said earlier. "We have tremendous challenges ahead, but there is hope. Anyway," he smiled as he clasped my hand, "I've always been an optimist."

Left: Temples and palm trees, Guyana is a melting point of cultures.

Martinique

Above: Compact and bijou: J.M. Distillery in Martinique.

Right: Everything must flow smoothly.

There is a real beauty about great machines. Maybe it stems from simple romanticism, a nostalgia for "traditional", pre-computerized days. Maybe it's just easier to understand this world of wheels, rollers, oil, cogs, and gears. It is real – vital. As I think this, I'm enveloped in a world of steam, vibration, and powerful, smooth-actioned energy. A thrilling sweetness fills the air. The whole scene reminds me of going to see the engines on board the paddle steamers which took us on holiday every summer down the Firth of Clyde – but this is rum-making, Martinique-style.

Rollers, studded with rows of tiny shark teeth, squeeze and strain the juice away from the cane. Every drop built up over the year is extracted, the spent, dry fibres carried up by conveyor to be the fuel for the boilers, to run the engine, to crush the cane, to heat the stills. Nothing is wasted in this great cycle of industry and nature. The big wheel keeps on turning.

Somehow, it seems appropriate that the French islands make rum in this fashion as, in many ways, it is one step closer to wine. Molasses can be stored, used when needed, bought from anywhere. Sugar cane juice must be used immediately; you

must be near the fields – take what the vintage gives you. The natural rhythm of it all ties these rums to the surrounding land. A producer such as J.M., coddled in its rain-forested glade, is an estate, a château of rum. It seems timeless, but *rhum agricole* – cane juice rum – is relatively new, commercially speaking. Since rum started as the by-product of sugar-making, molasses was used. No one, bar some moonshiners, would waste money by using that precious juice to make a spirit.

Yet *rhum agricole* is now Martinique's signature style, controlled by strict appellation regulations, elevating it to the same level of respectability as *Poulet de Bresse*, Morbier cheese or St-Emilion wine. Quite how this happened is a story of innovation, war, business, and politics. Pretty normal for rum.

In 1880, Martinique was home to 500 registered distillers, with the largest concentration around Saint Pierre on the slopes of Mont Pelée. Everyone made rum: the centralized sugar factories, small sugar-mill owners, and a growing number of independent distillers. This was one of Martinique's boom times. Thanks to the onset of the phylloxera vine louse in France, the metropolis needed a new spirit. Rum finally overtook sugar in importance.

That's not surprising. There was falling demand for Caribbean sugar, anyway, now that France had a thriving sugar-beet industry. Since the mother country no longer needed molasses or unrefined sugar, it made little commercial sense to continue production. Facing ruin, sugar planters and distillers began to make their rum from sugar cane juice instead, a practice that gained momentum after World War I, when beet returned. These innovators were headed by men such as Jean Neisson, Victor Depaz, Henri Dormoy, and the remarkable Homère Clément: a mulatto, a doctor, a radical politician, a plantation owner, and the father of *rhum agricole*. Today, his estate is open to the public, allowing you to wander around the elegant house that sits above the (now silent) distillery, framed by giant palms against a backdrop of blue cane.

It's a restful place, filled with ageing rum, with his bearded, gentle face on every barrel. The

Above: The idyllic habitation at Clément Distillery in Martinique.

silence of the island's warehouses is in contrast to the sheer energy of the rum-making process. It has an urgency to it, accentuated by the relatively small size of the distilleries. The bleeding canes giving up their brown juice; the heavy smell of the juice as it fizzes and hisses in its volcanic ferment; the bubble and steam of the various stills, each with their own subtle configurations… everything is linked. All pulling together in one space: a fusion of art, engineering, and nature.

La Carib Française

Martinique is totally different to the other islands yet strangely familiar, from the look of its sleek airport, the well-maintained roads (a rarity in the Caribbean), the fine food with rich sauces. Then it hits me: I'm in France, just with added bananas and sugar cane. It seems well-off, not in a glitzy,

way, but comfortable and middle-class: – like France herself. Yet while there is this blurring between French and Martiniquaise culture, it cannot be denied that rum, or *rhum* as it is known here, has been part of the island's soul for over 350 years. First as an energizing drink for slaves, then for the planters and, after the revolution, for French cities when a previous ban was lifted.

The island's middle history saw phylloxera give rum a lift, as did the Crimean War, when rum was shipped to the French Army as a morale-booster. The same thing happened in World War I, when the distilleries also worked flat out to make industrial alcohol for the military. The result was a mini-explosion of brands from négociants, based mainly in Bordeaux but also in Marseille, where Paulin Lambert, who went on to found St James,

was based. Though volumes declined after 1918, the subsequent two decades were when many of today's *rhum agricole* brands were founded.

Postwar successes

Life post-1945 was tough. With France slapping quotas on imports to protect its domestic spirits industry, many distillers went to the wall. The survivors of the 124 who were working in 1940, realized that they had to become self-sufficient in sugar cane and be willing to pay a premium for quality. Today, there are nine distilleries – Neisson, Depaz, J.M., St James, Dillon, La Favorite, Simon, Trois Rivières, and La Mauny – making seventeen brands (St James also produces Maniba, Madkaud, Hardy, and Bally; Simon makes Saint Etienne and Clément; Trois Rivières also produces Bernous and Duquèsne). The sole sugar refinery at Galion makes the molasses-based, high-ester rum known as *grand arôme*.

The French love to talk of terroir, the encapsulation of a sense of place in its wines: the effect of soil, sun, rain, and man's hand on a living thing. You can sense terroir in Martinique's greatest rums. The pungent hit of a fifty per cent ABV white takes you straight to this island's earth, a vegetal note mixed with that cane-juice aroma you smelled in the distillery that also brings flowers, light fruits, and, in J.M.'s case, a white pepper tree to mind. It doesn't try and win you over with its inoffensive, sweet lightness; it is bold, proud, and there in all its glory. Drinking it long allows it to be sipped at leisure, making that hit more acceptable.

Behind me, the Atlantic continues to break on the reef. Below in the town, someone is playing sax like Albert Ayler over a *gwo ka* drum beat. There, in the "real" Martinique, they are drinking it neat. Up here, I'm trying to drink every variant. But there's no right or wrong, no "us or them". The circle is widening. There are single-variety cane white rums; subtle, perfumed, aged examples; refined vintages. It's heaven. Tomorrow morning the engines will start again and the cycle will continue.

Slowly, the world is being drawn into it.

Guadeloupe

Sitting like a butterfly on the Caribbean waves, Guadeloupe also has (by Caribbean standards) a high concentration of distilleries. In fact, in purely volume terms, it makes slightly more rum than Martinique. Unlike that island, Guadeloupe has remained relatively untouched by mass tourism— although, this being a French dependency, you can rest assured that the hotels and restaurants are of a high standard.

While Martinique can be said to be cosmopolitan, Guadeloupe exhibits more of a calm, rural, air: a place where Creole culture has more of a say. Maybe it just conforms to our idea of what a Caribbean idyll should look like.

The island is divided into two distinct halves. The eastern part, Grande Terre, is flat, low-lying, and coralline. The western and less developed side, Basse Terre (the name means "windward" in old French), is volcanic. Still, there are plenty of distilleries to explore as you wind round its hills and tight bays.

The island's rum industry only really got going commercially with the outbreak of the oïdium mould and phylloxera louse in France, but from the word go, Guadeloupe has always always made more molasses-based *rhum traditionelle* than cane-juice derived *agricole*. That said, when the first great rum boom occurred in Martinique at the tail end of the nineteenth century, distillers there were reliant on supplies of molasses from their northern neighbour. Today, the split is more clearly defined. Although both islands made roughly 66,000 hectolitres of pure alcohol in the late 1990s, in Martinique eighty-five per cent of this was *agricole*. On Guadeloupe, only thirty per cent was made from cane juice, though as sugar continues its decline, the proportion of *agricole* is rising steadily.

It is these rums that are the island's finest. Every distillery makes an example. In fact, the majority specialize in it, leaving the production of *traditionelle* to plants such as Simmonet – which makes *agricole* during crop season and *traditionelle* for the rest of the year – and Damoiseau, the island's largest producer, which makes *traditionelle* for bulk shipments only.

All the rums (bar the small volumes of *rhum léger*, a light or highly rectified rum, which are made) are made in the standard French style, with single columns producing a spirit that is often of relatively low strength but with high levels of flavour. An exception is Montebello, whose linked columns create a lighter, more delicate spirit. In many ways, the difference between "French" column-still rum and standard column-still rum is like the difference between Cognac and Armagnac. While Cognac is made in pot stills, Armagnac uses small column stills to produce a lower-strength spirit packed with rich, full flavours which take many years to break down in cask. Not surprisingly therefore, all Guadeloupe's producers also produce *vieux* (aged) rums, which by law must be aged in barrels containing fewer than 650 litres for a minimum of three years. For me, some of the best come from the neighbouring island of Marie Galante, which, despite its size, still manages to pack in three producers: Magdala, Bielle, and Père Labat.

Guadeloupe *rhum traditionelle* has been a strong seller in France for many years, although its use has been mainly restricted to the kitchen rather than behind the bar. The battle now is to gain more awareness for and better appreciation of the *agricole* style, especially the aged versions. The rums are there; now what is needed is time, money, an appellation designation akin to that of Martinique, and a greater willingness to talk to the outside world. Once that happens, Guadeloupe will rightly be appreciated as a top producer.

Left: Time for a ti punch!

Barbados

Above: Not cannons, just stills, the Mount Gay Distillery in Barbados.

Right: Street life, Bajan-style.

It all starts here. For this rum traveller, landing in Barbados in the company of a 747 full of pallid British sunseekers is like coming home. This is as close as you can get to the home of rum, one of the places where you can touch on some of its deepest roots. From the airport, the tourists head straight for the south-coast beaches and I drive into the sugar cane fields. Machine harvesters are gorging themselves on the cane; tractors and trucks rattle and pitch over the patched-up roads to the sugar factories – one with the same name as my wife's Bristolian family.

The scale of the operation, where giant hoists and creaking conveyors take the stalks into the maw of the plant, is impressive. Yet sugar is dying. These days, the island's distilleries have to buy in much of their supply of molasses, although the Foursquare Distillery's straight-talking Richard Seale, for one, isn't mourning the end of an old culture. "Rum's image has been linked to sugar's," he says. "It has dragged us down. We should never be in the situation in the twenty-first century where all the value is added abroad. That old rum culture is dying because sugar is dying – and that's no bad thing."

Barbados was where English merchants first realized that they could make millions out of sugar. It was an almost mythic place, a fantastical, fertile island where fortunes could be made with virtually no effort. It soon became painfully fashionable. In *The Distiller of London*, a book published in 1639, there are two recipes for "Barbadoes Water", using the rind of Florentine citron, cinnamon, bergamot, cloves, saffron (for colour), rectified spirit, and sugar. You can read this in a number of ways: evidence of Barbados's fashionability, the first use of a large volume of sugar to pay homage to this magical place, but also as a strange precursor of rum – that sweet, spicy, amber-coloured spirit, that ghost from the future.

Barbadian rum today

Even if Jamaica and then Guyana overtook Barbados in volume, the island continued to make and export its rums, and like those two great rum nations, its distillers kept faith with tradition. Barbadian rum-makers have always retained their pot stills to give solidity and depth of flavour to their blends. The three distilleries working today – Mount Gay, West Indies Rum Distillery (W.I.R.D.), and Foursquare – have pot stills. W.I.R.D. also uses an old column configuration to produce a "heavy" mark, while Foursquare does the same by using two, rather than three, of its columns.

Yet tradition lives next to innovation here. At the time of writing, W.I.R.D. was getting new, modern fermenters, Mount Gay was expanding its barrel capacity dramatically, while at Foursquare, the Caribbean's most modern rum plant, there are closed fermenters for semi-continuous fermentations, vacuum stills, complex pot distillation, and experiments with different types of barrels. It is part of Richard Seale's passionate belief in rum's premium credentials and his total rejection of the industry's old, cap-in-hand approach to the major bulk buyers. Not that W.I.R.D. would agree, however. With its exclusive contract for the rum-based Malibu liqueur and as a major supplier to other big international brands, you can see why.

Link and legacy

Barbados runs on rum. As Bajan radio journalist David Ellis said to me one night: "Sugar and rum are inextricably linked to our psyche. Rum is crucial to our sense of identity." He points to a bottle of Mount Gay. "There's more to this brand to us than meets the eye. Because of our colonial past, because of slavery…" His voice dropped as if the next thing he said of was not to be overheard. "You see, this rum is *black*. It's ours and its success internationally is a big story."

Mount Gay's founder, Aubrey Ward, was a white planter who allegedly fathered ninety children (though some say it was closer to a hundred) When he died, he left his estate to them all. The St Lucy distillery is still run by his son, Carl. David's pride in the brand is because of this, not just because the brand has become international (thanks to drinks giant Rémy-Cointreau, which now has a controlling stake in Mount Gay), but because of how the Wards have stayed true to their roots and helped the people. It is local; it is international.

At a Mount Gay event, a government minister spoke in a witty, self-deprecating manner about rum. In the warm, thick night he talked of how difficult it is for small nations to survive in a globalized marketplace, and how important it is to have a brand out there with the map of the nation on its label. David, Clement from the Fisherman's Pub, and I went up to the bar, ordered another rum, and toasted the Wards.

But I was thinking also of the other merchants: the Seales, Valdemar Hanschell, the Fields, and the Doorlys, who kept Barbadian rum moving forward. In 1906, a law forbade distillers bottling their rums in containers of less than ten gallons. Bridgetown merchants simply bought rums, blended them, and slapped their own names on the label. Many of these brands are still alive today: Mount Gay, which appeared officially in 1926, Hanschell Innis's Cockspur, E.S.A. Fields, and Doorly's – the last two now both owned by Richard Seale.

So, my Bajan friends tell me, the tourist dollars are still flooding in, but we all know how fickle that industry can be. Rum, though; rum is our soul, and our rum is known in the world. Barbados is finally tearing up that map in Richard Ligon's book (*see* page 15) which outlines "the tenn Thousande Acres of Lande which Belongeth to the Merchants of London". We're dealing with post-colonialism, the building of pride and self-belief and how rum is the key. This isn't some commodity, like sugar, they say, but our core, our blood, our pride. Sugar is old money; it still represents slavery. As Bajan poet Kamau Braithwaite writes of his motherland:

for she wears on her wrist
the shadow of the chain

Strange thoughts, perhaps, in a place where the sea redefines turquoise and the feeling is one of total relaxation. Even the taxi drivers take their time here. People say hello to you out of sheer friendliness. It is a place of hummingbirds and doves, of ludicrous wealth, of slowly sizzling tourists, of the high-glitz lifestyle.

Barbados is multi-layered. One night it could be chilled Chardonnay, tuna sashimi, and mahi-mahi as the dark waves susurrate against the white sand; the next it could be the raucous fish-fry at Oistin's. You can chill at the plantation house of Villa Nova or drive to the wave-battered Atlantic coast in search of rum shops, places where you can buy your groceries while drinking ice-cold Banks beer in the afternoon heat and stun yourself with Fields' white rum. Then a new Barbados appears. The cricket is on, the domino tiles crash and clack in the back room. You can weave your way through this, looking for clues, trying to dig a little deeper into Barbados' porous, coralline limestone.

I sit and think of Mount Gay's Jerry Edwards and his gentle grace, the way his rums mirror his personality. They, too, have a subtle complexity. I think about Richard Seale's passion and radical visions, of how Barbadian rum has combined easygoing gentleness with a steel in its soul – and how its future is bright.

Left: A Bajan hoe-down.

St Lucia

In the mist of the sea there is a horned
island with deep green harbours ...
a place of light with luminous valleys
under thunderous clouds...
Her mountains tinkle with springs among
moss-bearded forests

Ever since I first read Derek Walcott's *Omeros*,
I have wanted to visit the Nobel laureate's
birthplace – and the setting for that epic poem.
He paints a vivid, multi-layered picture of an
island swept by rain, of deep forest and hawser-
like lianas; a volcanic land of sulphur, surf, and
deep-blue hills peopled by fishermen, ex-pats,
and *obeah*-women, all trying to find a place in
this world. It is about a sense of place and also of
displacement: the classic Caribbean dilemma.

The island does not disappoint. It is a place of
intestinal roads winding through rainforest, with
views into deep valleys and impossibly beautiful,
palm-fringed harbours; of the weird Pitons,
Walcott's "horns", which stab from the ocean; of
banana plantations and rum shops where people
stop every Friday night to lime (hang out), washing
their fried fish down with Bounty rum or the shop's
own special spiced-up specialty. This usually
contains some Dominican *bois bandé,* which has

an alleged aphrodisiac quality. Needless to say,
anything with this bark in it is a big seller, and
St Lucia Distillers, ever quick to see a niche and fill
it, uses it in two of its products: 7th Heaven and
Kwèyòl. Does it work? "You'll have to ask someone
older than me!" seems to be the universal answer.

On my way to the island, I was reading an article
on marketing in which the author recommended
that her students shouldn't just say, "This is a
banana" but *"What is* a banana?" It sounds
ridiculous, but her point was that only by looking
at the different ways in which you can look at a
banana (or any product) will you be able to sell it
successfully. It's something chairman Laurie
Barnard and his team at St Lucia Distillers have
been doing for a number of years. They're not just
selling rum; they're asking, *"What is* rum?"

Divide and multiply

The key to the firm's approach is differentiation,
aka niche-marketing. The company currently
produces twenty-one products: spiced rums,
flavoured rums, rum-based cream liqueurs and
sirops, as well as "straight" rums from the gentle
Bounty to the deep, toasty Admiral Rodney and
(my favourite) the complex, elegant Chairman's
Reserve. If Barnard has his way (and you get the
feeling he usually does), there's plenty more to
come. He'd like to plant cane to produce an
agricole style, is toying with the idea of organic
rum, and has just bought a new pot still.

Like virtually every rum producer, St Lucia
Distillers faces a dilemma. It has a solid bulk
business which it's reluctant to give up, but realizes
that, to prosper, it must not only become branded
but, as a small firm, differentiate itself from its
rivals. The advantage is that rum is so under-
exploited and so versatile that we're not even
talking about niche marketing. There's a bloody
great runway of opportunity open to the spirit.

Strangely, the island of St Lucia has only relatively
recently begun to appreciate its home-grown
product. Despite the normally fierce rivalry among
islands, ten years ago the largest-selling
rum here was Barbadian. Why? Laurie Barnard is

Above: A national symbol.

Right: Fisherman's pirogues
ready to go.

Trinidad

Above: Drink long, drink deep!

Right: A flaming good idea – the preparation of barrels.

Stay clear of the "Madness", Alex had told me. Not that I paid a blind bit of attention to his warning – to my instant regret. The pepper sauce ignited in my mouth and left a flaming trail down my throat. I could hardly taste the spicy chickpeas, but it didn't stop me asking immediately for another "doubles". That's Trinidad for you. It makes you do ridiculous, reckless things, just for the sheer fun of it. There are few places in the world where people seem to take such pleasure in just being alive. "Boy, do they know how to party," said one St Lucian friend. "Yes, they party," chipped in a Barbadian acquaintance. "They party and we work." Few in Trinidad would disagree. They see the Bajans as impossibly straight.

That's not to say they don't take their rum seriously. Not just in the quantities they consume, but in their approach to making it. This is a land where multiple column stills rule. Standing at the foot of the Angostura Distillers' multi-storey construction, you squint up into the sun, trying to follow the maze of pipes that wrap themselves around the soaring silver columns, trying to make sense of it all. This isn't one of those sticky, rustic plants that

are dotted throughout the rum-making world. This is rum-making as science, which has been Angostura's approach since the 1940s. A talk with production director Patrick Patel is filled with references to Puerto Rico's Pilot Plant (*see* page 77), gas chromatography, mass spectrometry, capillary columns. This is serious business, where, as Patel puts it, "The nose is allied to scientific investigation."

A bitters experience

It was perfect for Angostura when eighty per cent of its production was high-quality, light-flavoured bulk rum. Bacardi had a controlling stake in the firm until 1997, and most of the Bacardi sold in the Caribbean came from here. Was there any need to build international brands?

Then there was the bitters. Walk into Angostura's offices and that familiar smell hits you immediately: utterly exotic, all-permeating. You can't escape it. There's a bottle on every table in the staff restaurant; even the coffee gets a splash (something I'd heartily recommend) – and that's before you get to the drinks. Where would bartenders be without Dr. Johann Siegert's aromatic bitters? Strange to think that this idealistic Prussian first made it to help cure the debilitating fevers suffered by the troops of Simón Bolívar, to whom he was surgeon-general.

Siegert's sons moved the business to Trinidad in 1875, and, after World War I, diversified into rum. Not that the world knew it. We had forgotten that Trinidadian rum was the inspiration for the Andrews Sisters' "Rum and Coca-Cola", when American servicemen did their best to drain the island's stocks during World War II. It's the last line of the chorus that seems the most relevant today, the one that goes "working for the Yahnkee dollaaaah". Not just "Yahnkee" in Angostura's case, but the Bacardi dollar– not to mention the British pound. And that is the firm's problem, especially with the free market just around the corner and the ending of subsidies. The decision has been made. Angostura is going branded.

Other Caribbean Islands

Above: The author hitches a ride.

Right: A prize catch.

King Cane no longer rules the Caribbean and the old symbiotic relationship between sugar plantation and rum distillery has changed in recent times. The sugar cane fields have disappeared from some islands, and rum distilling has gone the same way. First the cane went, then the rollers and boilers fell silent, the fermenters emptied, the yeast died, the stills cooled, and with them went a small piece of the islands' heritage and culture. Sugar might be an international commodity, but rum speaks of its place – made from local ingredients and influenced by climate. It was crafted and cared for by local people, and made in a style they enjoyed.

At the time of writing, the sugar crisis has forced many islands to seek out new, more profitable earners and grub-up their sugar cane fields. Bauxite, light industry, spices, but most of all, tourism, have usurped King Cane. But you can still make rum without home-produced molasses; you just import it. Rum blenders can keep a brand alive, or create a new one, by buying stocks from distilleries on other islands. At least by blending a rum on an island, some of that place's spirituous heritage is retained. Bermuda is a case in point. It

has no sugar cane, no distillery, but still, proudly, has its own rum: Goslings Black Seal. Carriacou has its fearsome Jack Iron, made in Trinidad. The Caymans' Tortuga Rum Company makes its range by blending Jamaican and Barbadian (or "Bajan") rums.

St Kitts is slightly different. There is a distillery here, yet it didn't make rum but high-strength cane spirit sold as C.S.R. (Cane Spirit Rothschild). The plant is now run as a joint venture with Guyana's Demerara Distillers, but is not producing. Quite what happens next isn't exactly clear.

Local heroes

What is clear is that, cane or no cane, every island, every rum shop, wants to keep its rum alive. Thankfully, distillers are a stubborn breed. There is something about seeing that clear, innocent-looking liquid trickling out from the still, its just-born aroma mingling with the perfumes of the island, that inspires them to carry on, no matter what the obstacles.

A perfect example of this, and of how rum is often the victim of the sugar market's vagaries, is the story of the St Vincent Distillery. One of the islands that was left, for a short time, in control of the Caribs, St Vincent was tussled over by France and Britain until it was annexed by Britain in 1763. Sugar, while an important part of the agricultural mix, never became a monoculture; indeed, mountainous St Vincent was considered a "barren island" (in sugar-production terms), and other crops such as arrowroot began to gain in importance. That's not to say sugar plantations weren't established though by the end of the century sugar had collapsed and many of the field workers migrated to Cuba.

In 1963, the old Mount Bentinck Estate distillery, which had been built in 1900, changed its name to St Vincent Distillers. It spoke of a new beginning for rum from the island, but '63 was the very year that St Vincent's cane fields were uprooted in favour of bananas. Inevitably, the sugar mill closed down, but imported

molasses could be used for rum-making – and
still is these days.

The Caribbean islands are at the mercy of world
trade. By the 1980s, bananas from small plantations
on islands such as St Vincent could no longer
compete with those coming from the vast,
US-controlled estates in Central and South America.
So, back came the cane, in went new equipment
to the distillery, and in 1985, rum made from local
molasses was once again flowing from the two-
column still. I reckon you have to have a supreme
sense of irony to live on this island, because by the
time the first truly local rum was being made again,
the mill had closed, the cane was being uprooted
and bananas were going back in!

That's enough to make most people give up, but
thankfully, the Greaves family, who bought the
distillery in 1996, are made of tougher stuff. Rum,

you see, is part of the lifeblood of St Vincent. It
speaks of the island's history, from Carib times to
now. It must survive. As it does in Dominica. This
densely wooded, mountainous island was also left in
control of the Caribs before being annexed by the
British in 1763. Like St Vincent, sugar was never the
sole crop. During the eighteenth century, all the
cane was replaced by coffee. This lack of reliance on
sugar is shown by the fact that, by the end of the
nineteenth century, it only made up fifteen per cent
of its export earnings. But no matter; rum remained.
Today there are two estates. Belfast's Red Cap
brand is a blend of rums from Guyana, Trinidad, and
Barbados, but the Machoucherie Estate, owned by
the Shillingford family, not only makes its rums from
Dominican sugar cane (grown on the estate), but,
unusually for a "British" island, from cane juice.
Antiguan rum's story might be slightly different,

but a similar theme of enlightened, stubborn locals preserving their heritage also runs through it. Rum was probably made here soon after the first cane was planted around 1650; contemporary accounts suggest it was made in a "light" style (for its time). By 1764, there were 300 plantations on the island; by 1897, 15,000 acres of cane were being processed in seventy-eight factories. By 1939, there were two.

The fertile island of Grenada has managed to retain a rich rum-making tradition while some of its neighbourrs have struggled. Grenada is a living rum museum and while the island's biggest and best-known brand, Clarke's Court, is produced from a "modern" two-column set-up, the island's other distilleries still belong to privately owned estates, such as River Antoine, Westerhall, and Dunfermline.

Grenada's fertility means there is none of the mono-culture so prevalent in the rest of the Caribbean. Cocoa, fruits, and spices are all grown, as is cane, allowing the estates to be self-sufficient in cane syrup for their pot-still rums.

What goes around...

Centralization may have made economic sense, but as the factories closed, the distilleries fell silent, reducing the number of rums local bar owners could blend and spice up into their own brands. By 1932, a group of them decided to buy some plantations and build their own distillery. Their Caballero rums – an aged and a white – were both made in pot stills from muscovado molasses, though the pressure to make light, dry rums for the US market in the 1950s saw the pots replaced by a copper column still and a change of name: from Caballero to Cavalier and in time the release of the English Harbour export range. They are wonderful rums, though I can't help wondering what difference muscovado molasses would have made and what the pot still would have done.

But things never stay the same, in life or distilling. These days, there's no more sugar cane on the island, tourism drives the economy, and it, in part, is driven by rum. Come to think of it, maybe some things never change after all.

South America

For most of us, rum is a Caribbean product, a sweet distillation of the laid-back lifestyle of tropical islands, yet Latin America produces more spirit from sugar cane than anywhere else. Although it might not all be classified as rum, it remains the spirit of choice from Mexico to Patagonia. With the exception of Guyana (*see* page 82), stylistically Latin American rums fall into the light, gentle "Spanish" style first perfected in Cuba and Puerto Rico. The sugar-cane brandies (*aguardiente*) are lighter still and, in cachaça's case, a different sub-section of rum entirely. But more of that later.

Mexico

The early Spanish settlers may have been more keen on gold than sugar, but sugar cane was an early crop of the young Mexican colony. While technically it was illegal to distil in the days of mercantilism, the colonists were soon applying those ancient Moorish techniques to any crop they produced, be it grain, fruit or cane, to give to their slaves. However, the fact that this crude rum began to be sweetened (and sometimes spiced) into a drink called *chinguirito* infers that the settlers were beginning to drink it themselves as an alternative to

Above: Fresh produce successfully tempts the eye.

Right: Music and rum are the perfect partners.

the brandies from their homeland. What is certain is that it would be many years before they would try and distil the fermented juice of the agave cactus, known as *pulque*, to make mezcal.

Mexico is still a consumer of cane spirit. The country produces well over ten million proof gallons a year and the drink still outsells Tequila. There's no coincidence that, when Bacardi began to expand from its Cuban base, Mexico was the first country in which it built a distillery (in 1929). Almost four decades later, Seagram followed in its footsteps and built a massive distillery in Ixtapaluca, near Mexico City.

Today, there are a mass of producers of *aguardiente de cana* (and blends of *aguardiente* and mezcal) including Bacardi whose Ciclón rum/tequila mix has appeared recently. Domestic rum producers include Huasteca (Potosí) from the River Valles, and Veracruz from the sugar-growing region of Córdoba. In the latter, the Spanish heritage is retained though the use of a *solera* system for aging the rum. When the rum, say, the six-year-old, is bottled, half of the volume of the oldest brandy is removed from the six-year-old barrels. The missing volume is then topped up with three-year-old rums, which are ageing on a higher floor. They, in turn are topped up with one-year-old rum, and those barrels are refreshed with new spirit.

This method of fractional blending was first perfected in Jerez, Spain, (coincidentally near to where the first recorded distillation took place in Moorish Spain) and ensures a consistency of product. Technically, it means the age statement on the label often isn't strictly accurate, as there will be traces of the rums which were put in cask when the *solera* was established.

Guatemala

For some reason, whenever I uncork a bottle of Zacapa Centenario, people give me a funny look. It could be the wickerwork cover that encases the bottle, but I suspect it is because to Brits, rum just shouldn't come from Guatemala. Yet one sip and they know they are tasting one of the great rums of the world.

During its colonial period, Guatemala was better known as a coffee producer. Though rums were produced, it wasn't until last century that commercial distilleries were established. Licorera Guatemalteca (1914) was one of the pioneers, with the other main producers (Zacapaneca, Quezalteca, Euzkadi) appearing in the 1930s.

Like any small country heavily reliant on agriculture and in need of foreign earnings, postwar Guatemala saw the sense of merging these firms into one centralized organization, the slightly unromantic-sounding Industria Licoreras de Guatemala. What it lost in romance it gained in improvements in plant and a dramatic upward shift in quality. Today, the firm accounts for virtually every bottle of rum that is drunk in Guatemala, which may in turn account for the

fact that Zacapa Centenario was a closely guarded secret until recently. With an average age of twenty-three years, this rum is aged in what the firm describes as a double *solera* in warehouses that sit at 7,650 feet (2,332 metres). Whether it is the *solera*, the older barrels, or the cool temperature offsetting the problems associated with tropical aging, the result is exceptional – though it does overshadow the excellence of La Nacional's other brands such as Botrán and Colonial, all of which have that stylish, elegant, sweet, gentle Latin American nature.

Nicaragua

I first came across Nicaragua's Flor de Caña when it provided liquid refreshment for a variety of pro-Sandinista events in Bristol. Salsa, jazz, and copious amounts of Nicaragua Libres lubricated

the fund-raising nights held after Somoza was deposed and this small country was trying to rebuild itself.

One night I tried it on its own. It was a revelation. Here was a rum that was so delicate, so ethereal and charming that I never mixed it ever again. The firm that makes it and an equally impressive range, Compañía Licorera di Nicaragua, was founded in Chichigalpa in 1890, though it moved into commercial rum production only in 1937.

The distillery, which started with pot stills, was revamped in 1963 and once more between 1994 and 1996, signalling a more aggressive international marketing push. In common with most Latin American rums, all its rums are aged; even the white is given four years in barrel. I'm hugely impressed with the technical control, but I don't think of five column stills when I taste this. I'm back in Bristol, when the world seemed alive with possibilities.

Ecuador

Rum is made in virtually every South American country, from French Guiana (*see* Guadeloupe, page 91), Surinam, and Guyana (page 82) to Colombia, Peru, Bolivia, and Argentina. Ecuador is no exception. The country still has five plants in production, the most important of which is Desarrollo Agropecuario, which is based in the cane fields of the Azuay Valley.

The firm's San Miguel brand first appeared in the late nineteenth century from the plantation. By the turn of the last century, Desarrollo Agropecuario, like many others, had decided that rum, rather than sugar, was a sounder option financially and bought in UK-made stills. These days, the stills, close to the cane fields of the Guayas river plain, are Italian, but as with Guatemala, the aging facilities are high in the mountains: in Cuenca, some 2,300 metres (7,546 feet) above sea level. The key to these delicate, classy rums, like so many in this lighter style, lies in the blending of different ages of rum rather than the creation of different marks. One to watch.

Two other South American countries stand out not just for their rum production but for the simple fact that, without them, much of the Caribbean rum industry would collapse. With the Caribbean sugar industry in a state of turmoil, the rum world is increasingly reliant on Venezuelan and, more importantly, Brazilian molasses, a fact that makes many seasoned rum industry personnel just a little twitchy.

Venezuela

Venezuela's place in the history of alcohol is less to do with rum and more to do with the fact that it was here, in 1823, that Simón Bolívar's doctor combined roots, barks, and spices to create medicinal bitters. The alcoholic base he needed was provided by local rum. Though Angostura moved to Trinidad in 1875, Venezuela continues to be a major rum (and sugar) producer. Two of its major producers, Carupano (which supplies the rum for Mexican brand Baraima) and Santa Teresa, were originally sugar plantations in the late eighteenth century, the former in the eponymous valley while Santa Teresa is in Aragua.

Venezuela is a major liquor market, not just for rum but for Scotch. No surprise, then, that giant multinational Diageo has an interest in Pampero, though former Canadian drinks company Seagram was first in through its joint venture with Licoreras Unidas (Cacique). The Canadian influence is obvious in the set-up of the distillery, which claims to be the only one in South America besides Guyana to produce heavy, pot-still rums – as well as marks from batch and continuous columns. Pot-still rums are seen at their best in the top-end Diplomatico Reserve.

Brazil

Brazil produces much of the world's molasses and is the largest producer of sugar cane, but strictly speaking, its best-known spirit isn't a rum; it's cachaça. In fifteenth-century Bahía, a fermented sugar-cane drink (*garapa doida*) was being poured like pig swill into wooden troughs and fed to slaves and livestock. Meanwhile, in the south of the country and gold mines of Minas Gerais, stills were beginning to be introduced. Soon, the two were put together, and cachaça was born, both as a form of barter to buy slaves and to keep them intoxicated while their Portuguese masters sipped fine Madeira. Today, Brazil runs on cachaça. The numbers are frightening. The biggest brand, 51, sells fifty million six-bottle cases a year, making it the second-largest-selling spirit brand in the world.

There's some confusion as to why cachaça isn't a rum and how it is made. It can be made from cane juice, sugar syrup or molasses. The large commercial brands (51, Ypioca, Velha Barreira, 3 Fazendas, Pitu, Tautzinho, etc) are highly rectified in column stills. After distillation, the spirit is blended and reduced in strength with sugar syrup and water and then filtered. The best are clean and quite sweet; the poorest are rough and industrial.

Production of traditional cachaça (such as Germana) is significantly different. Here, fermentation is triggered by a starter made from cane juice and maize, which creates a mixed spirit and not, therefore, a rum. The wash is then distilled either in pots or column stills and can be aged. There's a similarity between them and some French rums; that slightly earthy, vegetal note is always present. But sod the technicalities: pick a good one from either camp, grab some limes, batter them into submission with some sugar, throw in some ice cubes and a slug of cachaça and dream you are playing beach football with Ronaldo.

As Brazil tries to get its economy back on track, so molasses and cachaça will provide important export earnings. From being a Brazilian specialty, cachaça is now being promoted globally, and the caipirinha is an international star cocktail. The best brands in Minas Gerais now operate their own quality-control system, part of a shift by producers to promote not just quality but more sensible drinking within Brazil. Abuse of cachaça is a problem, yet the root of this doesn't lie with the drink, but with poverty. By bringing in foreign currency, cachaça may in fact be part of the solution. Complex – but isn't rum always that way?

Left: Drinks of the favelas.

Jason and I were eyeing up the building when the Cuban security guard beckoned us over. "You want to go on the roof?" he asked. No second invitation was needed. Inside was a perfectly preserved art deco lobby. Some dusty chairs sat where a bar had been. From the roof terrace we had a panoramic view of Old Havana. A sculpture of a bat cast its shadow across the city.

It was here that the Bacardi family planned their global takeover, here that they looked down on a Havana that was filled with Americans immersing themselves in the hedonistic delights of Cuba's capital. Just down the road is the Floridita; opposite the Plaza, the Sevilla can just be seen. All are legendary bars: the places where Bacardi first sealed its reputation, but which haven't stocked the product since 1961.

Bacardi's story starts with Don Facunado and the search for a lighter style of rum. At a time when rum-making was often crude and the distillate heavy, Don Facunado Bacardi used improved technology, science, and natural talent to make his rum. In 1862, he and his partner, José Bouteiller, bought the Nuñez distillery in Santiago de Cuba. Don Facunado isolated a yeast strain (still used today), used an English-built still with rectifying plates above the pot, and filtered his rum. All of these steps played their part, but Bacardi then went one step further than his competitors. He and his family believed in branding.

By 1910, the company was bottling in Barcelona; eight years later it was doing the same in New York. Bacardi took advantage of the tax breaks offered by the US government and, in 1936, built a distillery in Puerto Rico, where its Cuban-style rums, you feel, helped to initiate the establishment of the Rum Pilot Plant (*see* page 77). Today, Bacardi owns four distilleries: in Puerto Rico, the Bahamas, Mexico, and India. And the company makes one hell of a lot of rum – 180 million litres are sold every year.

Ask how it is made and the polite response is: "We ferment. We distil a light and heavy style.

We filter; we age; we blend." That said, for all its use of state-of-the-art technology, ultimately the "secret" of Bacardi comes down to the art and skill of its blenders.

They have been working overtime recently. There's a new range of flavoured rums, a Tequila/rum mix called Ciclón, and hints that investigations into wood are about to bear fruit. Ironically, Bacardi has built its reputation on not being thought of as a rum, but as a brand. That strategy is now changing. As the rest of the industry begins to explore new niches, so Bacardi needs to reassert its heritage. This is not only good for rum, but for the firm as well.

Bacardi wasn't the only brand to disappear post-Revolution. In the early 1870s, brothers Benjamin and Eduardo Camp had emigrated from Spain to the southern city of Santiago de Cuba, and within two years had blended a new rum brand: Matusalem. In time, the Alvarez family, who were by now related to the Camps by marriage, took charge. By the early 1950s, Matusalem was claimed to have a fifty per cent share of the Cuban market. Like the Bacardis, the family left Cuba after the Revolution.

Today, Claudio I. Alvarez, the great-grandson of the founder, is running the show from the firm's headquarters in Florida, although its brands, a blend of Caribbean rums, are produced in the Dominican Republic(!). Like many Latin American rums, Matusalem utilizes a *solera* ageing system. While some old Cuban brands are still alive, sadly the same cannot be said for rums from the continental USA, where just two distilleries carry on the old heritage of American rum-making. One, Prichard's, is in Tennessee; the other, Celebration Distillation, makes its home in Louisiana.

The British style

Captain Morgan, named after the seventeenth-century pirate-governor of Jamaica, was created by Sam Bronfman's Seagram company as part of its major postwar blitz on the international drinks industry. A Jamaican arm, Captain Morgan

Right: Lords of all they surveyed: Bacardi's old Havana H.Q.

Distillers, was founded in 1945. A year later, the firm was also producing in Puerto Rico; for a time it owned a controlling stake in Puerto Rico Distillers, where it produced the Ronrico brand. Over the years, Seagram's rum empire would include distilleries in Jamaica (Long Pond and then Monymusk), Mexico (Ixtapaluca), and Hawaii (Leilani), as well as joint ventures in Venezuela (Cacique), Costa Rica (Gran Blasón), and Brazil (Montilla).

If most new rum consumers in the USA think of Captain Morgan as a spiced brand from Puerto Rico, for British and Canadian drinkers it is one of the old, dark rum brands which dominated the market in the 1960s and '70s. These brands were part of a tradition dating back to the late eighteenth century, when rum brokers began to blend marks from British Guiana, Jamaica, and Barbados. The style was influenced not just by the marks available, but by the brokers' biggest customer, the British Admiralty.

On the high seas

Rum had been given to sailors in the British Navy from 1655 simply because the drinking water on board ship was so foul. By 1733, however, an official rum ration was part of the daily routine on board, though Admiral Vernon ("Old Grog") ordered that the half pint a day should be issued in two servings – and diluted. By 1850, a quarter-gill per day became the approved measure. By this time, rum had become firmly embedded in British naval life, and a standardized style had emerged: a Demerara-based blend assembled by the Navy's oldest broker, E. D. & F. Man.

The rum ration came under increasing attack as twentieth-century technological advances put new pressures on a modern navy. On Saturday, August 1, 1970 (known in naval circles as "Black Tot Day"), the ration was abolished altogether, although the spirit lives on, thanks to Chuck Tobias, who bought the rights to Pusser's Rum from the Admiralty (*see* page 81).

One of the earlier naval suppliers was Cornishman Lemuel (aka "Lemon") Hart. His eponymous Jamaican blend is still made by Allied-Domecq and is due to celebrate its 200th anniversary in 2004, pre-dating most of the UK's main "dark" rum brands which appeared in the mid-nineteenth century.

The latter include brands such as George Watson's OVD, now owned by Wm. Grant, and United Rum Merchants' (U.R.M.) Black Heart. U.R.M. was founded in 1946, when three old blending and broking firms – Alfred Lamb, (whose eponymous blend was created in 1865), White Keeling, and Portal Dingwall & Norris – merged. A year later, it became part of sugar giant Booker and was amalgamated into Allied-Domecq in the early 1990s, though by then the days of a head-to-head clash with Captain Morgan via saucy calendars and high-spending marketing campaigns had long gone.

The world has moved on. As has Seagram, which is now out of the drinks business completely, having sold its rum assets to the giant Diageo corporation. Yet there is hope for "British-aged" rums with the creation of a premium rum sector. This was pioneered by whisky bottler Cadenhead, and in recent years it has been given a massive boost by a range of aged, single-still and single-distillery rums from Bristol Spirits. Ironically, these appeared as a result of dark rum's decline when brokers were left with massive overstocks. Most went to the wall, but Ben Cross' Main Rum Company persevered and found itself in a market where there were nice parcels of old rums, no brokers, and a growing interest in premium spirits. In Bristol Spirits' John Barrett, Cross found a kindred spirit, and the firm's range of marks from across the Caribbean is a hugely exciting development for the industry, showing that rum, too, has its own equivalent of malt whisky.

Germany and Rumverschnitt

All the major European ports were rum centres and Germany's were no exception. From the mid-eighteenth century, its rum industry was centred around the Baltic port of Flensburg.

Left: The original coconut rum, the piña colada.

Northern Germany's love of real Caribbean, and especially Jamaican, rum came to a halt in 1900, when import duties on rum were hiked in order to protect the home distilling industry. The solution was the creation of the high-ester style (*see* page 43), which allowed the German rum blender to take what was basically a rum concentrate, add it to *Korn* (grain) and call the resulting product *Rumverschnitt*. This is now in contravention of the EU rum regulations and the style is being phased out, although it did damage the image of genuine German brands such as Pott.

The situation in Austria was even worse. Its *Inlanderrum* contained virtually no rum at all, while the "rums" from eastern and central Europe were made from sugar beet – again, an illegal practice under EU law.

Réunion and Mauritius

There is a third, French-owned, rum-making island, this time situated in the Indian Ocean. Réunion has been producing the spirit since 1704, although there is evidence that the slaves were drinking a fermented cane-juice drink, *fangourin*, prior to stills arriving. A boom in sugar production in the late nineteenth century resulted in an increase in the number of distilleries, though Réunion soon found itself at the mercies of the sugar-beet industry. Even so, there were still thirty-one distilleries operating in 1928. Today, there are just three.

Unlike Martinique, it was those rum-makers independent of the sugar industry who suffered most, though increased centralization of the sugar industry also played its part. Of the three surviving Réunion distilleries, two (Savanna and Rivière du Mat) are owned by sugar firms and a third, Isautier, remains family owned. The rums are made in the *traditionnel* style, although a tiny amount of *agricole* is also produced, most of which appears to be consumed on the island.

Rivière du Mat is the largest of the producers. A semi-continuous fermentation yields a *vesou* with a strength of around ten per cent ABV, which is then distilled either in a three-column

still for a lighter style, or an old single-column for a heavier mark. It is a similar story, still-wise, at Savanna, though this plant makes more *rhum leger* than *traditionnel* and also produces *rhum grand arome* and some *agricole*. The tiny Isautier distillery makes only 4,000 H.A.P. (*hectolitres alcool pur*), mostly *traditionnel*, and has an extensive range of barrel-aged rums, all of them *agricole*. All the Réunion rums are available in France.

Rum is also made in Mauritius which, like Réunion, experienced a boom during the nineteenth century (there were thirty-seven distilleries here in 1878). Today, there are only three producers on the island, with brands including the light, sweet Blue Bay from the Medine distillery in Bambous, and Old Mill, an *agricole* style made by Grays & Co.

India and Nepal

Though fermented sugar drinks have been made in India for millennia, commercial rum distillation is a relative newcomer to the subcontinent. Production is dominated by the massive Ajudhia Distillery, while distiller/blender Shaw Wallace makes the Mutiny brand. Both are rarely seen outside India.

Nepal Distilleries is, however, taking the export route with its Khukri brand. Established in Kathmandu in 1960, the rum is molasses-based and distilled in a three-column still, although the firm feels that it is the maturation process in vats made from Himalayan timber which gives it its character.

The Philippines

Like India, the Philippines was growing cane long before it ever reached the Caribbean. Yet rum production only started (with the Spanish) in the eighteenth century, and only became large-scale and quality-oriented from the mid-nineteenth century onwards, thanks to distillers such as Domingo Roxas and Joaquim Elizalde. The latter's firm, Tanduay, evolved into the country's best-known rum producer internationally, although the domestic market is dominated by La Toneda.

Australia and New Zealand

Strange as it may seem, Australia, too, has had a long association with rum. Indeed, it was a form of currency in the early colonial days, when it was used to pay convicts for their labours. Those first settlers would have drunk imported rum or else made their own moonshine; the first commercial Australian rums weren't produced until 1860, when Beenleigh begin distilling with a double-pot system which was eventually joined by another pot that had been used in a distillery hidden in the hold of the *SS Walrus*! Today, only Beenleigh and Bundaberg, founded in 1888 and now owned by Diageo, make rum in Oz. With ninety-five per cent of the dark rum market in Australia, "Bundy" is the country's second-largest-selling spirit.

More recently, New Zealand has joined the world of rum-distilling. The South Pacific distillery, which makes the Roaring Forties brand, started life in a converted Queenstown garage in 1982 but is now ensconced in a larger facility in Nelson.

Spiced and flavoured rums

Go into any rum shop in the Caribbean and you'll find a bottle or, more likely, a shelf-load of bottles all crammed full of berries, pods, barks, and fruit. Spiced rum is as old as the spirit itself; spicing it up was one way to hide the flavour of badly distilled spirit, while the ingredients used often doubled as medicines – adding them to alcohol increased the efficacy.

As rum evolved, so spiced rums became a way for rum shops to differentiate themselves. All you needed was some overproof rum (higher alcohol gives greater extraction), your ingredients – vanilla, nutmeg, fruits, or barks such as the allegedly aphrodisiacal *bois bandé* – and you could create your own secret brand.

It wasn't until the 1980s that brands began to explore the spice world, among them such big-hitters as Captain Morgan and Bacardi. For me, though, the best commercial brands are those made by smaller distillers such as St Lucia's Kwèyòl or, best of all, Foursquare's Spiced. Both have natural flavours, the room-filling aromas, and tingling exoticism of the greatest rum-shop examples, but with greater consistency and availability though you can always try it yourself.

From spiced rum it was a logical step to making a flavoured rum. That in itself meant choosing a flavour which not only went with rum, but one that immediately said "Caribbean". I've long hoped that Lang's Banana was the first, but the evidence seems to suggest that it was Diageo's (now Allied's) coconut rum, Malibu, which is now the second-highest-selling rum in the world.

Where Malibu went, others followed, including Koko-Nut, Koko-Kanu, and Parrot Bay. Then Cruzan opened the market still further with its range of naturally flavoured rums: pineapple, mango, vanilla, etc. Bacardi hit back with Limón as well as a range of newer flavours, while St Lucia Distillers came in with Crystal Lime and a range of rum-based cream liqueurs, a tack also tried by Wray & Nephew.

Rum purists might look down their noses at these products, but they are missing the point. The flavoured rums have appeared for two reasons: rum's versatile flavour, which melds beautifully with a vast range of ingredients, and its trendiness and appeal to a new generation of drinkers and bartenders.

"I do see rum coming back," says Allied's master blender Steve Hoyles. "Although the younger drinker might not like traditional rums, people are growing out of blandness. It is up to us to make rum different: to change the profile, make it exciting, and play up that Caribbean heritage."

Left: Banana rum, anyone...?

Rum is the most versatile spirit in the world. No other drink can match its diversity of styles and flavours. It can be white, or aged, made in pot stills or columns. It can be spiced or flavoured. It works as an after-dinner sipper with a cigar or as the perfect base for a cocktail. There's a world of rum out there to be discovered. But what should you look for?

How to taste rum

Forget the notion that you only taste or "nose" rum. You do much more than that. In fact, you put *all* your senses to work: sight, smell, taste, hearing, touch – plus that remarkable reference bank in your head known as memory. Nor do you have to be an "expert". All it requires is patience and practice.

Ideally, your rum tasting should take place in a well-lit room which is free from any smells – flowers, cooking food, etc. – that can obscure the aromas. You shouldn't wear perfume or aftershave, or smoke during the session – unless you are doing a rum and cigar tasting, that is.

If possible, use a tasting glass. A tulip-shaped sherry *copita* is perfect for this, as is a brandy snifter, or even a white-wine glass. Tumblers might be great for drinking, but they don't concentrate the aromas like the sloping sides of a tasting glass do.

Try to taste a number of rums at the same time, using a familiar one as a reference point. Having a comparison to hand allows you to differentiate more easily and helps with those tricky descriptors. If you are trying a number of rums, taste them in a logical order. In general, try to move from clear to dark, light to heavy, young to old, weak to strong, and low- to high-ester.

Have some still mineral water on hand to dilute the samples. Water helps to release the volatile aromatic compounds which are held in the spirit, opening up the rum and allowing you to detect more subtle aromas. Finally, relax. If you can't pin down a particular aroma, don't keep sniffing until your nose goes numb. Go on to the next sample. Above all, enjoy the experience; do it with friends and listen to their comments. This often helps spark ideas off in your own mind.

So just how do you use your senses in a rum tasting? First, look at the clarity of the rum. It should be bright. The colour can give an indication of how long it has spent in cask. In general, a rum that has spent a long time in wood will be dark amber, maybe mahogany, in colour. A greenish rim gives an indication of age and shows that the rum has not been heavily caramelized. If you tilt the glass away from you and then slowly bring it back up, you will notice its "legs": the liquid lines that cling to the side of the glass. These indicate the viscosity of the rum. In general, the thicker and more slow-moving they are, the heavier and more full-bodied the rum. Think of the inside of the glass as being like the inside of your mouth; a thick-legged rum will probably be a pretty chewy experience.

Now sniff the rum, just above the rim of the glass. Note the first aromas that appear; they are the central ones on which the rum's character is built. Are they light or heavy? Can you perhaps smell toffee, flowers, or fruits? Maybe they are spicy or oaky. If the rum is made from cane juice, you might pick up a vegetal note; if higher in esters, a pungent note reminiscent of pineapples, maybe even nail varnish, will swirl out to meet you.

After tasting the rum neat, add some water and smell it again. Think of those cardinal aromas and try and work out what kind of fruit they remind you of. Is it banana or mango, citrus or dried? What kind of spices – pepper, nutmeg, cinnamon? You may pick up some wood-derived aromas such as vanilla, coconut, or chocolate. Is the smell simple or complex?

You'll spend much of your time nosing. After all, the human nose can detect aromas in parts per trillion, and aromas have a powerful impact on our minds. Smells are gases which travel up the nose until they hit the olfactory epithelium and bulb situated bang between your eyes. From there, receptors carry the information to the brain, specifically to the limbic brain, which is the part that has the most to do with memory. This is why

when you smell something, a picture snaps on in your head. Aromas are loaded with memories, often from childhood. Revel in them, but if you're having trouble, then shut your eyes and try to think of a place it reminds you of, or perhaps what season. And share it. Don't be shy to say what you're smelling. Everyone's opinion is valid.

Tasting confirms what we have smelled. When you first taste the (neat) rum, hold it in your mouth to assess its weight, texture and primary flavour. Is it light, fresh or robust? Is the texture silky-soft or dry and hard, thin or mouth-coating? After adding water, taste it again and hold it in your mouth once more. Do those aromas still come through and are new ones appearing? What has happened to the complexity? Think of what the tastes and flavours are and where they occur: at the start, in the middle of the palate, and on the finish. The rum should grow, change, and evolve in the mouth. Finally, work out whether it is balanced; sweetness should be balanced by dryness and oakiness and vice versa.

Every time I taste rum I am amazed at what a remarkable spirit it is. Never forget that it is there to be enjoyed. It's a drink which puts a great big stupid grin on your face. Maybe it's the sugar; maybe it's the sunshine trapped in the cane. Maybe it is because, when you close your eyes, it takes you to the place of its birth: a distillation of turquoise seas, pounding surf, and clear skies, of a relaxed pace of living, of a love of life.

Rum and cigars

Great cigars and great rums have a natural affinity for each other. Just think for a moment of the aromas and flavours you get from rum and those you get from cigars. Cigars can be mild, rich or full-bodied – like rum. Their aromas can bring to mind cocoa, coffee, tanned leather, undergrowth, and wood. The flavours can remind you of fruits, liquorice, nuts, pepper, and spices, and they can even be sugary-sweet. Found any of those before? You bet: in great rum.

Crucially, what makes rum such a perfect partner with a good cigar is the sweetness of the spirit. You need complexity in order to cope with those rich flavours from the tobacco, but you don't want them in partnership with dry oak and too much grip. Instead, you need a spirit that will sweeten and complement the smoke.

So, what cigar do you choose? Let's say you're in a bar and order a mojito as your cocktail. It arrives: cold and refreshing, the mint waking up your palate. It would be silly to light up a *robusto* cigar. Rule number one: short drinks need short, light to medium cigars. A Romeo y Julieta Petit Prince (four inches x forty ring gauge), Cohiba Exquisito (five inches x thirty-six) or San Cristobal de La Habana El Príncipe would be the perfect match for most palates, though if you're intending to make this a session, something slightly larger would be an option. The medium-bodied, complex Hoyo de Monterrey Epicure No. 1 (five and five-eighths inches x forty-six) is a wonderfully versatile smoke. It works because the cigar doesn't dominate the cocktail, while the mint cleans the palate. As the smoke dissolves into the air, you are transported to Havana.

Rule number two: for an after-dinner drink, you'll want a fuller-bodied cigar and a richer, wood-matured rum. There are some rums which just seem to snuggle up to cigars better than others. The complex, rich spiciness of Appleton Extra is a perfect choice, while El Dorado fifteen-year-old is a mellow, elegant drink for a slow smoke, as is the silky, complex Havana Club 15, while Zacapa Centenario is for people who live life on the sweeter side.

And the cigar? I'm a Partagas fan, and find that the rich Series D No. 4 (four and seven-eighths inches x fifty) works well, as does the full-bodied Montecristo No. 2 (six and one-eighth inches x fifty-two). On the lighter side, there is that hugely reliable Hoyo de Monterrey Epicure No. 1, or even a Cohiba *robusto* (five inches x fifty). This is all about maximizing enjoyment. Light the cigar; let it smoke down for a couple of minutes while allowing your rum to warm up. Then bring them together in your mouth for a synthesis of the best the Caribbean can offer.

Cocktails

Rum has always been used in mixed drinks. The early planters drank it watered down with added sugar, a sprinkle of nutmeg, and maybe some fruit. Originally, this might have been done to hide a badly made spirit, but as rum's quality improved, it was still served mixed: in punches, in swizzles, juleps, fizzes, and flips. The reason is simple. That luscious, sweet taste gives a subtle undertow to any cocktail or punch. You can throw anything at rum and it will happily absorb it. You could say the same for vodka, but unlike that spirit, rum adds its own character to a drink – which is the very reason bartenders love it so much.

Ancient cocktails

While some of the early concoctions listed on this page might seem slightly alarming to us today, they were the staple drinks of the early American settlers, Caribbean planters, and English gentlemen. I'm indebted to John Hull Brown's *Early American Beverages* for some of these recipes. The punches quoted from Jerry Thomas's *Bartender's Guide* are the tip of the iceberg from this, the first cocktail book. As a nod to authenticity, measures here have not been converted to metric, and the "directions" are as originally intended. Good luck!

Classic Daiquiri (1898)

2oz gold rum

juice of half a lime

1 tsp sugar dash gomme syrup (or sugar syrup)

Shake and strain.

Medford Rum Punch (Jerry Thomas)

1 tbsp bar sugar, dissolved in a little water

1 half glass Medford rum

1 pony Jamaica rum

2–3 dashes lemon juice

1 slice orange

Rum Flip (1704)

Fill a large pewter mug two-thirds full of strong beer. Add molasses or sugar and 1 gill (quarter pint) of New England rum. Plunge a red-hot poker into the mix until it bubbles.

Rum Flip 2 aka Bellowstop

(Eighteenth century)

Make a mix of 1 pint cream, 4 eggs, and 4 pounds sugar. Fill flip mug two-thirds full of beer, add 4 spoonfuls of the mix, a gill of rum, and then insert red-hot poker.

Rum Punch 1

(from Charles Lamb's *Popular Fancies*)

12 lumps of sugar

1 pint hot water

2 lemons (juice and peel)

2 gills [half pint] old Jamaica rum

2 gills brandy

half gill porter

dash of arrack

Carefully stir... until it actually foams; and then Kangaroos!

Rum Punch 2 (1860)

Brew 1 pint of green tea, add sugar. Discard tea leaves and add liquid to the punch bowl. Add juice and oil from 2 limes Dissolve 2 tbsp guava jelly in 1 pint of boiling water then add:

6 glasses Cognac

2 glasses Madeira

1 bottle old rum

1 quart boiling water

sprinkle nutmeg on top

add sugar to taste

Tom & Jerry (Jerry Thomas, 1862)

Use a punch bowl for the measure

Take 12 eggs

half a small bar glass of Jamaica rum

1 half tsp ground cinnamon

half tsp ground cloves

half tsp ground allspice

sufficient white sugar

Beat whites of eggs into a stiff froth and the yolks until they are as thin as water, then mix together, add spice and rum and stir up thoroughly and thicken with sugar until the mixture attains the quality of a light batter. To serve in a bar glass: take 1 tbsp of the mixture, 1 wine glass of brandy, fill the small bar glass with boiling water, grate nutmeg on top, and serve with a spoon.

Modern cocktails

Here is a small selection of cocktails. There are some classics, mostly from the golden age of Cuban bartending – hence the need for Havana Club rum – and others with a modern twist. Tip: first learn how to make a daiquiri and then start improvising.

All measurements are in millilitres (ml); 30ml = 1oz = 2 tbsp, and all recipes make one drink. "Shake and strain" means shaking the ingredients in a cocktail shaker that is half-filled with ice-cubes. Then strain the liquid into a glass, retaining the ice in the shaker. Use fresh ice for every drink, but whatever you do, get shaking!

Añejo Highball
(Dale DeGroff, published in Gary Regan's *New Classic Cocktails*)

45ml Añejo rum
15ml orange Curaçao
15ml fresh lime juice
2 dashes Angostura bitters
ginger beer
1 lime wheel
1 orange slice (garnish)

Fill a highball glass with ice-cubes. Add all ingredients. Top up with ginger beer. Stir and garnish.

Between the Sheets

15ml each of: white rum, brandy, lemon juice, and Cointreau

Shake and strain into a cocktail glass.

Caipirinha

1 lime
60ml cachaça (Germana or Samba & Cana)
3 sugar lumps

Cut the lime into wedges and muddle with sugar in an Old-Fashioned glass. Fill the glass with ice and pour in the cachaça. Stir and serve.

Caipiruva
(Dale DeGroff)

As with the Caipirinha, but use Samba & Cana and substitute fresh green grapes for the lime.

Centenario

45ml Appleton V/X
30ml Wray & Nephew Overproof Rum
8ml Kahlua
8ml Cointreau
dash grenadine
juice of one lime
sprig of mint (garnish)

Stir ingredients with ice in a highball glass. Garnish with mint.

Corn and Oil

Stir together:
30ml ESA Field's White Rum
30ml Taylor's Velvet Falernum
dash of Angostura bitters

Pour over crushed ice.

Cubano Centenario

15ml Havana Club Añejo
30ml Havana Club 3 Años
15ml triple sec
8ml white crème de cacão
30ml fresh lime juice
1 tsp grenadine

Stir ingredients with ice in a highball glass.

Daiquiri No. 1
(Constante Ribalagua)

1 tsp sugar
juice small lime
60ml white rum

Mix everything in a blender with crushed ice and strain into a cocktail glass.

Daiquiri No. 2

Same as No. 1, but with 1 tsp of fresh orange juice and a dash of orange Curaçao.

Daiquiri Frappé

30ml Havana Club White Rum
juice small lime
2 dashes maraschino liqueur

Blend for 20 seconds over crushed ice, then serve in a large cocktail glass with ice.
NB: All daiquiris can be made in this way, or strained.

Daiquiri Hemingway

15ml fresh lime juice
8ml maraschino liqueur
8ml grapefruit juice
60ml Havana Club White Rum

Blend over crushed ice and serve.

Daiquiri Mulata

1 tbsp white sugar
8ml lime juice
15ml dark crème de cacão
8ml unsweetened grapefruit juice
45ml Havana Club Añejo 7 Años

Blend over crushed ice and serve.

Dark and Stormy

1 half oz Goslings Black Seal Rum
4oz ginger beer
lemon or lime wedge

Serve in a highball glass.

Fire and Ice

(Anguela Anagnostou)
50ml rum
10ml Licor 43
15ml lime juice
50ml Coco Lopez
1 inch fresh chilli (reduce according to taste)

Blend all ingredients well, then add crushed ice and re-blend.
Serve in a piña colada glass and garnish with a chilli.

Floridita

45ml Havana Club White Rum
15ml sweet vermouth
dash white crème de cacão
dash grenadine
juice of half a lime

Shake and strain into a cocktail glass.

Glen's Moijito

(Glen Hopper)
1 lime
Mint leaves
2 tsp brown sugar
1 small piece of fresh chilli
60ml Appleton Special
ginger beer
chilli and a mint sprig (to garnish)
3 drops Tabasco, optional

Muddle all the ingredients in a 16oz glass. Add crushed ice and top up with ginger beer.

Honolulu Cooler

90ml gold rum
1 tsp sugar
dash gomme syrup (or sugar syrup)
juice 1 lime
2 dashes raspberry sirop

Shake and strain into a cocktail glass.

Innocent Foreplay

35ml Foursquare Spiced Rum
30ml chilled espresso
30ml rock candy syrup
60ml milk

Shake all ingredients together with ice, strain into a martini glass, top with heavy whipped cream mixed with Grand Marnier, and top with orange zest.

Knickerbocker

60ml white rum
15ml crème de framboise
15ml orange Curaçao
dash of fresh lemon juice
pineapple wedge (garnish)

Shake and strain into a cocktail glass.

Mai Tai No. 1

30ml white rum
15ml Cointreau
8ml Rose's Lime Cordial
45ml orange juice
45ml unsweetened pineapple juice
splash grenadine
15ml gold rum
wedge of pineapple (to garnish)

Shake together the first five ingredients and strain into a highball glass half-filled with ice. Add the grenadine and gold rum. Stir. Garnish.

Mai Tai No. 2

60ml gold rum
30ml orange Curaçao
45ml Rose's Lime Cordial
15ml orgeat syrup
1 tsp gomme syrup (or sugar syrup)
splash grenadine
15ml Wray & Nephew Overproof Rum
Wedge pineapple & wedge lime (to garnish)

Shake and strain the first five ingredients into a highball glass half-filled with ice. Add the grenadine and overproof rum. Stir. Garnish.

Marmalade Fashioned

(Barry Chalmers)

50ml Appleton V/X
1 tsp marmalade
4 dashes Pechaud's bitters
orange (garnish)

Stir the marmalade and bitters into an Old Fashioned glass until the marmalade melts. Then add the rum gradually.

Mary Pickford

45ml Havana Club 3 Años
45ml unsweetened pineapple juice
1 dash grenadine
1 dash maraschino liqueur
lime twist (garnish)

Shake and strain into a cocktail glass.

Mojito

mint leaves
half tsp gomme syrup (or sugar syrup)
juice of half a lime
60ml Havana Club 3 Años
soda water
dash Angostura bitters
sprig of mint (to garnish)

In a Tom Collins glass, muddle the mint leaves with the sugar and the gomme. Add the lime. Half fill glass with ice. Add rum and top up with soda water. Add a dash of Angostura and garnish with a sprig of mint.

Nuff Rum

(Anguela Anagnostou)

20ml Wray & Nephew Overproof Rum
25ml Stone's Green Ginger Wine
10ml Limoncello
5ml peach syrup
3 dashes each Angostura and orange bitters
orange and lemon twists (to garnish)

Build over ice-cubes in an Old Fashioned glass.

Passion

(Chris Edwardes, UK)

30ml Bacardi 8yo
15ml crème de pêche
juice 1 lime
15ml gomme syrup (or sugar syrup)
30ml passion-fruit purée
Champagne

Shake all the ingredients (apart from the Champagne); strain into an ice-filled highball glass. Fill with Champagne and serve.

Piña Colada

60ml white rum
30ml coconut cream
60ml unsweetened pineapple juice
4 chunks fresh pineapple
pinch of salt

Blend until smooth and pour into a piña colada glass.

Pear Daiquiri (Frappé)

30ml white rum
1 quarter oz pear schnapps
30ml fresh pear purée
30ml fresh lime juice
dash gomme syrup (or sugar syrup)

Blend ingredients together with some crushed ice. Pour into a large cocktail glass and serve.

Raspberry Mint Daiquiri

60ml white rum
handful fresh raspberries
6 mint leaves

Muddle the raspberries and mint in the shaker. Shake and strain into a cocktail glass.

Rumbo Jam

(Katy Keck, published in
New Classic Cocktails)
90ml light rum
60ml pineapple juice
45 ml cranberry juice
15ml fresh lime juice
1 tsp fresh ginger juice

Shake and strain all ingredients into a highball glass filled with ice cubes.

Sun-Downey

(Jonathan Downey)
40ml Havana 3 Años
15ml Campari
15ml Cointreau
15 ml fresh lemon juice
lemon twist (to garnish)

Shake and strain into a cocktail glass; garnish.
Or serve over ice.

Ti Punch

90ml *rhum agricole blanc*
1 tsp gomme syrup (or sugar syrup)
1 lime
chilled water

Lightly muddle a wedge of the lime with the gomme syrup in an Old Fashioned glass. Add the rum and stir. Drink as a shot, then have a large glass of the chilled water.

Tre

(Asa Nevestveit)
40ml Havana Club
5ml gomme syrup (or sugar syrup)
5ml Chambord liqueur
20ml apple juice
Lemon twist (garnish)

Stir and strain into a cocktail glass. Add the garnish and serve.

Wray Smash

(Barry Chalmers)
50ml Wray & Nephew Overproof Rum
2 strawberries
half a peach
10ml peach liqueur
10ml fraise liqueur
10ml lemon juice
3 mint leaves
10ml gomme syrup (or sugar syrup)
Mint sprig (to garnish)

Muddle all ingredients together and shake. Serve over crushed ice in an Old Fashioned glass.

There is no single thing as "rum". There are rums for sipping, others for mixing. Aged rums, overproof rums, pot-still, continuous-still, single-casks, flavoured or spiced. No other spirit has this diversity of flavour, depth, and breadth of quality. What has emerged from this book just reinforces that point. The more you taste, the clearer stylistic signatures became. The subtle lightness of Puerto Rico and St Croix; the delicate sweet style of Cuba, South America, and Trinidad; the balance of Barbados; the mellow subtlety of Guyana; the elegance and lift of Jamaica; the grip of old vintage rums of Martinique; the apparently ageless UK-aged rums and, yes, those treacle-toffee notes of those old "navy" brands. Dive in, find some old friends and meet many new ones. This is just a taster. Enjoy!

Scoring

These rums have been tasted not just by producer, but also stylistically – like with like – and marked accordingly. The stars are there only as a guide.

✪	Poor
✪✪	Average
✪✪✪	Good. I'd be happy drinking this
✪✪✪✪	Excellent
✪✪✪✪✪	Superb

But please: read the notes which, hopefully, explain how the score was given. Words are more important than scores!

Admiral Rodney (St Lucia)

Owned by St Lucia Distillers
Castries, St Lucia
St Lucia Distillers is one of the most innovative rum-makers in the Caribbean, with a portfolio targeting (and creating) every possible niche in an expanding market. With columns and two types of pot stills, it appears to have all bases covered.
Tel: +758 451 4258
Fax: +758 451 4221
Email: info@sludistillers.com
Website: www.sludistillers.com

Admiral Rodney

40% ABV

✪✪✪✪

Colour/Nose: Amber. Pot-still power comes through along with tobacco, tea, chocolate-covered raisins. Dry with good complexity.
Palate: Soft. Like all the firm's rum, sits nicely on the palate. The weighty, pot-still character is balanced by gentle oak.
Finish: Rounded and soft.
Conclusion: Big and mature.

Alleyne Arthur (Barbados)

Owned by R. L. Seale
Foursquare Distillery, St Phillip, Barbados
Alleyne Arthur was an old Barbadian rum bottler whose brand-name is now owned by R. L. Seale.
Tel: + 1 246 420 1977
Fax: + 1 246 4201976
E-mail: rumfactory@sunbeach.net
Website: www.foursquarerum.com

Alleyne Arthur's Old Brigand

40% ABV

✪✪✪

Colour/Nose: Gold. Soft and clean with dried sage, honey, coconut matting, lime. Has character.
Palate: Soft, gentle start. Decent grip. Coconut and orange notes.
Finish: Light grip.
Conclusion: Great light-/medium-bodied mixer.

Alleyne Arthur's Old Brigand Black Label
40% ABV

✪✪✪✪

Colour/Nose: Amber. More robust and mature. Bay leaf, spices, ash. Sweetness moving into toffee crisp, apricot. Punchier, with gingery notes.
Palate: A touch of smoky oak helps give great feel. Has rich weight in the mid-palate. Light herbal (lavender) flavours. Mellow and sweet.
Finish: Balanced.
Conclusion: Exciting, spicy. Great on its own.

Alleyne Arthur's Special Barbados Rum
43% ABV

✪✪✪

Colour/Nose: Old gold/amber. Light- to medium-bodied with turmeric, vanilla, and a little citrus fruit. Summery.
Palate: Soft and clean with light wood. Chewily attractive.
Finish: Tingling.
Conclusion: Lovely balance. Good mixer.

Angostura (Trinidad)
Part of C. L. Global Brands
Port of Spain, Trinidad & Tobago
Founded in 1824 as a producer of aromatic bitters, Angostura Distillers is a firm that has taken a scientific approach to rum-making. For many years it exported its rums as bulk, but today it is at the forefront of the international development of Caribbean-owned brands.
Tel: +868 623 1841/5
Fax: +868 623 1847
Email: icss@angostura.com
Website: www.angostura.com

Angostura White 3yo
40% ABV

✪✪✪

Colour/Nose: Clean, light, and dry with light citric notes (lime), hints of apple and pear, and some old-fashioned lemonade.
Palate: Light, bone-dry, and clean. Banana and apricot. Good feel.
Finish: Short.
Conclusion: Well-made, light rum.

Angostura Gold 5yo
40% ABV

✪✪✪(✪)

Colour/Nose: Gold. High-toned with very light oak notes: coconut, clove, lemon peel; with water, a little vanilla. All very delicate.
Palate: Clean, soft, and delicate: tropical fruits, green mango, banana. On the light end of the scale with a hint of heavy spirit in the middle.
Finish: Light spice.
Conclusion: Once again, a lovely pure spirit. Good mixer.

Angostura Dark 4yo
40% ABV

✪✪(✪)

Colour/Nose: Dark indeed with caramel-toffee, sweet banana, and coffee notes. In the house style, but a little "covered".
Palate: Silky feel with touches of vanilla, custard cream, ripe banana. Chewy, if a little bland.
Finish: Slight bitter edge.
Conclusion: Well-made, clean spirit, but not as good as the Gold.

Angostura Añejo
40% ABV

✪✪✪

Colour/Nose: Full and sweet. Lots of moist coconut, tropical fruits and a light, smoky note.
Palate: Rounded, soft, and sweet. Coconut all the way.
Finish: Soft.
Conclusion: Made in Venezuela; has excellent South American sweetness and lightness.

Angostura 1919 8yo
40% ABV

✪✪✪✪

Colour/Nose: Gold. More serious, with some heavier spirit adding richness and extra complexity. Still light and sweet, however, with vanilla, guava, light, spicy wood, and baked apple touches. Gorgeous.
Palate: Creamy, soft, and mellow. Milk chocolate and spice. Light to medium-bodied. Subtle.
Finish: Soft, quite complex.
Conclusion: A light, elegant rum. Shows huge promise and finesse. Highly recommended.

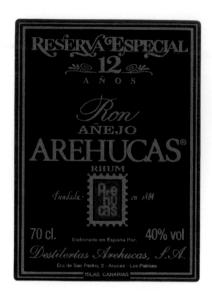

Angostura 1824
40% ABV
✪✪(✪)

Colour/Nose: Plain weird aromas: old wood, fresh varnish, shellac, floor polish, prunes, and incense.
Palate: Has a certain exotic, velvety quality. Spice then vanilla. Old and odd.
Finish: Slightly bitter.
Conclusion: Almost trying too hard. The 1919 is the route to take.

Appleton (Jamaica)
Owned by Wray & Nephew
Nassau Valley, Jamaica
The first record of rum production at Appleton Estate was in 1749. It has been part of the Wray & Nephew portfolio of rums since 1916. Recently upgraded, it makes pot- and column-still rums.
Tel: +876 963 9215/6/7
Fax: +876 963 9218
Email: appleton@infochan.com
Website: www.AppletonRum.com

Appleton White
40% ABV
✪✪✪

Colour/Nose: Clear and bright with a clean, crisp nose that has hints of lime and lemon.
Palate: Soft and smooth: banana sweets, vanilla, a little light coconut. Gentle.
Finish: Clean, then dries nicely.
Conclusion: Good feel as much as aroma. A sound base for a mixed drink.

Appleton Special
40% ABV
✪✪✪(✪)

Colour/Nose: Gold. Light honey and sweet apple mixed with nut, rich tea biscuit, and a light, smoky, char note.
Palate: Fresh and gently sweet. Good balance between soft fruit, orange, and a gentle nuttiness (macadamia and Brazils).
Finish: Sweet and clean.
Conclusion: One of the lighter Jamaican blends. A great cocktail rum.

Appleton V/X
40% ABV
✪✪✪✪

Colour/Nose: Amber. Balanced and clean with maple syrup, vanilla, toffee, cocoa, tangerine marmalade, and a ripe banana, apricot, grassy, spicy lift. Balanced.
Palate: Soft and lightly chewy, with banana, nutmeg, and a touch of pecan. Balanced oak.
Finish: Lightly spicy.
Conclusion: Drink solo or mixed. Versatile.

Appleton Extra
43% ABV
✪✪✪✪✪

Colour/Nose: Rich amber with coppery glints. Rich, pot-still weight hits immediately. Becomes increasingly complex: honey, spices, dried fruit, Seville orange, sweet tobacco, and tanned leather.
Palate: Unfolds beautifully with classic Jamaican lift. Chocolate, sweet fruits, and balanced, dry oak. Full weight. Ripe, mature, and elegant.
Finish: Tobacco, nutmeg, and orange peel.
Conclusion: One of the great rums of the world.

Appleton 151 Proof
75.5% ABV
✪✪✪

Colour/Nose: Tan/crimson. Hot with good intensity; earthy, vegetal, banana, cane juice.
Palate: Savoury. Touches of leather, date, wood.
Finish: Currant and plum.
Conclusion: So strong it even carries a warning on the back label to keep it away from naked flame. NOT a session drink!

Arehucas (Canary Islands)
Arucas, Las Palmas, Gran Canaria
The Canaries were a major sugar producer long before the Caribbean was exploited, and rum is still made there today. The distillery in Arucas, in the north of Gran Canaria, was established in 1884.
Tel: + 928 600 050 / 54 / 58
Fax: + 928 603 913
E-mail: destilerias@arehucas.com
Websites: www.arehucas.com; www.arehucas.es

Arehucas Oro

37.5% ABV

OO

Colour/Nose: Amber. Lightly floral and sweet. Fades in the glass quite quickly.

Palate: Light, sweet. Attractive and soft, if a little fragile.

Finish: Very light.

Conclusion: A decent mixer.

Arehucas Añejo 12 Años

40% ABV

OOO

Colour/Nose: Amber. Polished wood, resin, pine sap. A light note of violet and spices. Again, the aromas tend to fly off.

Palate: Perfumed again with good evidence of natural oak ageing. Soft, sweet spirit.

Finish: Nutty.

Conclusion: Haunts of sweet beeswax scents.

Bacardi (International)

Nassau, Bahamas (head office)

San Juan, Puerto Rico (main distillery)

The behemoth of the world of rum with four distilleries worldwide and sales in excess of twenty million cases a year.

Website: www.bacardi.com

Bacardi White

40% ABV

OO(O)

Colour/Nose: Light, clean and soft with very light sweet/floral notes and hint of banana. Dry.

Palate: Dry with good balance. Soft in the middle. Light.

Finish: A nodule of sweetness.

Conclusion: Well-made but strangely un-rum-like.

Bacardi Gold

40% ABV

OOO

Colour/Nose: Gold. Clean, light, quite fine-bodied: passion-fruit, dried peach, butterscotch.

Palate: Soft with gentle, quite honeyed feel. Slightly chewy with pulpy fruits (apricot)

Finish: Sugar, cashew.

Conclusion: A gentle, well-made mixer.

Bacardi 8yo

40% ABV

OOOO

Colour/Nose: Old gold. Quite perfumed, with evidence of maturity: orange peel, honey, caraway, aniseed, mint. Light oak. Very clean.

Palate: Mix of sweet spices with ripe apricot and banana. Medium-bodied, gentle and poised.

Finish: Soft and mellow.

Conclusion: A really lovely rum. Proof that Bacardi can compete at the upper end. More, please!

Bacardi Limón

35% ABV

OO

Colour/Nose: Clean and bright. Lemon zest/oil but ever so slightly dirty.

Palate: Sweet with floral notes alongside the lemon. Medium-dry palate…

Finish: …but a sugary finish.

Conclusion: Average.

Bacardi O

35% ABV

OO

Colour/Nose: Clear, bright. Orange concentrate; water shows a more zesty character.

Palate: Very zesty, almost spicy, but still retains that slightly confected air.

Finish: Flat. A bit dull.

Conclusion: Average.

J. Bally (Martinique)

Owned by Rémy-Cointreau

Le François, Martinique

Bally began making *rhum agricole* in 1917 in the town of Carbet. Noted for its aged rums, distilled at the St James distillery.

Tel: + 596 596 69 53 36

J. Bally Blanc

50% ABV

OO(O)

Colour/Nose: Clear, bright. Light with blossom, cane juice and berry fruits. Hint of pea pod.

Palate: Light, dry, fresh, and clean.

Finish: Slightly hot.

Conclusion: Delicate, fair.

J. Bally Vieux
45% ABV
✪✪✪✪

Colour/Nose: Amber. Fine, even slightly lean. Amaretti biscuits, apple, graphite, and cedar. Has real finesse.
Palate: Shows a very restrained, pure character with honeyed cane sweetness all the way.
Finish: Nutty.
Conclusion: A refined rum.

J. Bally 7 Años
45% ABV
✪✪✪

Colour/Nose: Rich copper. Elegant. Richer than the *vieux*, with cream, sultana, and hints of light cigar tobacco. Light notes of honey and balanced oak.
Palate: Hazelnut, honey; cedar and apple wood.
Finish: Dry; slightly too grippy.
Conclusion: A bigger but firmer example.

J. Bally 1992
45% ABV
✪✪✪✪(✪)

Colour/Nose: Dark amber. Rich and mellow, moving into beeswax, and notes of balanced wood, cantuccini biscuits, and graphite. Ripe.
Palate: Prunes. That waxy character fills the palate out. This is honeyed and deep, with great balance.
Finish: Long.
Conclusion: Rich, very stylish.

J. Bally 1990
45% ABV
✪✪✪✪✪

Colour/Nose: Dark amber. Richer and more concentrated than the 1992. Quite fat, even, with toffee and raisin hints plus a touch of beeswax. Dried apricots/cling peaches. Some sweet spices. Complex.
Palate: Full (for *agricole*), showing a good interplay between sweet and savoury. Wonderful balance.
Finish: Nutty.
Conclusion: The wonderful thing about this type of rum is that you feel you can taste the differences between vintages. Fascinating.

J. Bally 1989
45% ABV
✪✪✪✪

Colour/Nose: Amber. Rich. Sweet notes of popcorn and lemon balanced by older, funkier ones: mushroom, truffle, chocolate.
Palate: Soft. Balanced oak and good grip, though slightly austere.
Finish: Crisp. Orange.
Conclusion: Halfway between the '92 and '90.

J. Bally 1979
45% ABV
✪✪✪(✪)

Colour/Nose: Amber. Mature and elegant, with hints of plum brandy. The most fragile of the range.
Palate: Soft still, and mouth-filling with toffee in the centre.
Finish: Long.
Conclusion: Subtle and old.

Barbancourt (Haiti)
Port au Prince, Haiti
Founded in 1862 by Dupré Barbancourt and now owned by the Gardère family. A cane juice rum but made in a manner more akin to a Cognac (double distillation, French oak). The star of Haiti.
Fax: + 509 09 23 63 55
Websites: www.barbancourt.com; www.todhunter.com

Barbancourt 3 Star, 4yo
40% ABV
✪✪✪✪

Colour/Nose: Pale gold. This is fresh and light, with notes of barley-sugar, mead, apple, and currants and a hint of acacia. Shows a waxier note with water.
Palate: Light, but filled with flavours and a silky texture. Touches of spiced syrup with hazelnuts, orange peel, Turkish delight dusted with sugar. Fine-bodied.
Finish: Nutmeg and cracked pepper put in an appearance.
Conclusion: A sophisticated kind of drink. Light but well-balanced.

Barbancourt Special Reserve 5 Star, 8yo

40% ABV

✪✪✪✪✪

Colour/Nose: Pale gold. Refined, complex nose of honey, green apple, praline, and a vinous note like Sauternes. Sweet but delicate with a nutty edge.
Palate: Soft and silky but with extra weight and complexity. Apricot jam, barley-sugar, nougat, cane juice, ginger. Subtle and delicate.
Finish: Ginger. Honey.
Conclusion: Balance is the key to great rum. This has it – and how.

Barbancourt 15yo

43% ABV

✪✪✪✪

Colour/Nose: Richer, more toasty, with notes of ash and dried leaves but still that elegant nut and honey signature. Spicy with dried fruit.
Palate: One step along from the 5 Star, but still very fine and elegant rather than big and burly.
Finish: Nut and praline.
Conclusion: Just refined, elegant rum.

Bermudez (Dominican Republic)

Santiago de los Caballeros, Dominican Republic
An old, family owned Dominican Republic producer that has been producing rums in the mountain town of Santiago since 1852. Best-known on the home front but beginning to appear abroad.
Tel: + 809 581 1852
Fax: + 809 226 1852
E-mail: ja.bermudez@codetel.net.do
Website: www.bermudez.com.do

Bermudez Don Armando

40% ABV

✪✪✪(✪)

Colour/Nose: Amber. A sweet nose with sultana, burnt orange peel, toasty oak, red fruits, and a herby lift. More melted toffee with water.
Palate: Quite light and creamy with a good tingle of spice; then the fruit surges through. Good weight. Clean and delicate.
Finish: Soft and light.
Conclusion: Very well-made.

Bermudez 150 Aniversario

40% ABV

✪✪✪(✪)

Colour/Nose: Amber. Good weight moving into treacle and honey; some hickory, roasted almond, and sweet paprika notes from wood. Becomes almost sherried with date and walnut.
Palate: Sweet with toffee, custard and nuts. Quite stylish.
Finish: Nutty and spicy, then some sweetness.
Conclusion: Again, well-blended. One for sipping after dinner.

Bermudez Limón

35% ABV

✪✪((✪)

Colour/Nose: Light, with a lime tint. The fresh nose is a mix of lime and bitter lemon, or old-fashioned lemonade. Quite fat.
Palate: Sweet and pretty sugary, although there are some almost bitter oils. Decent zestiness, but a bit artificial.
Finish: Tingling.
Conclusion: Lacks balance.

Black Cat (Surinam)

Controlling interest held by Angostura Paramaribo – Suriname
Produced by Surinam Distiller Handelmaatschappij, which was founded in 1966 and is now part of the ever-growing C.L. Global Brands Group. Not exported.
Tel: + 597 47 33 44
Website: www.blackcatrum.com

Black Cat

40% ABV

✪✪✪

Colour/Nose: Pale gold. The nose is unusual but strangely appealing, with the nuttiness of peanuts or toasted rice. Similar to a fine arrack.
Palate: Soft, with hints of toasted rice and apple. Musky. Soft feel.
Finish: Light. Clean.
Conclusion: This comes right out of left field and shows real character.

Black Cat Limón
40% ABV

ooo(o)

Colour/Nose: Vibrant. Lemon tart and cream.

Palate: Good weight. Very fresh. Lemony.

Finish: Lemon rind.

Conclusion: Zingy and clean. Good.

Black Heart (UK)
Owned by Allied-Domecq
London, UK

Big-selling Caribbean blend that has been a major seller in Scotland since the 1850s.

Tel: +44 (0) 20 7323 9000

Email: www.allieddomecqplc.com

Website: www.allieddomecqplc.com

Black Heart
40% ABV

oo(o)

Colour/Nose: Treacle-dark. A thick aroma with burnt toffee and soft, dried fruits.

Palate: Light to medium-bodied with a thick, quite rich mid-palate.

Finish: Dry.

Conclusion: A classic old Scottish style.

Bloomsbury Spirits (UK)
Owned by Royal Mile Whiskies
Bloomsbury, London, UK

Tel: +44 (0) 20 7436 4763

Fax: +44 (0) 20 7436 4764

Email: info@royalmilewhiskies.com

Website: www.royalmilewhiskies.com

Pot Still Demerara 1992
(aged in Laphroaig casks)

46% ABV

ooo(o)

Colour/Nose: Amber. Deep, pot-still weight. Cooked apple, raisin bread; some floral notes.

Palate: Medium bodied and slightly smoky. Ripe and funky. Hint of fig and prune.

Finish: Light smoke.

Conclusion: I presume this comes from the same batch as Cadenhead version (*see* page 145) but this has much more to it.

Blue Bay (Mauritius)
Bambous, Republic of Mauritius

An Indian Ocean rum produced in secrecy (*i.e.* they won't tell me!). Now beginning to be exported.

Tel: + 230 452 0400

Blue Bay White
40% ABV

oooo

Colour/Nose: Incredibly fruity impact that's like being in a rum distillery in full swing: cane juice, passion-fruit, melon, banana grove, and some vegetal/grassy notes. Rich and oily.

Palate: All these fruits, plus a light, nutty grip. Mouth-coating, oily, and sweet.

Finish: Soft and gentle.

Conclusion: A great characterful white that's brimming with flavour.

Borgoe (Surinam)
Controlling interest held by Angostura
Paramaribo – Suriname

Borgoe rum was introduced in 1982 to commemorate the one-hundredth anniversary of the sugar estate and distillery at Marienburg.

Tel: + 597 47 33 44

Website: www.borgoe.com

Borgoe 82 (Surinam)
38% ABV

ooo

Colour/Nose: Gold. Very perfumed: maraschino cherry, apple, toasted rice. A little artificial.

Palate: Creamy, soft, and clean. Has good feel.

Finish: Dry.

Conclusion: Pleasant enough.

Bounty (St Lucia)
Owned by St Lucia Distillers
Castries, St Lucia

Tel: +758 451 4258

Fax: +758 451 4221

Email: info@sludistillers.com

Website: www.sludistillers.com

Bounty Gold

40% ABV

✪✪✪(✪)

Colour/Nose: Gold. Light and clean on the nose, but with hints of some richer spirit: sultana, lime, ginger, dried ripe banana, papaya.

Palate: Clean, soft, and quite light but with personality and good feel. Honey, sultana, banana loaf.

Finish: Light.

Conclusion: Very good balance. A very good mixing rum.

Bristol Spirits (UK)

Wickwar, Gloucestershire, UK

This firm is at the forefront of a new movement to do for rum what malt whisky has for Scotch. It makes small batches (sometimes single casks) of aged, single-still or single-estate rums, sometimes finished in a different type of oak. Individuality and character are the keys here. One to watch for the future.

Tel: +44 (0) 1454 299 880

Fax: +44 (0) 1454 294 572

Email: bristolspirits@btclick.com

Website: home.btclick.com/bristolspirits

Bristol Spirits, Gardel 10yo

(Limousin oak finish; Guadeloupe)

46% ABV

✪✪✪✪(✪)

Colour/Nose: Amber. Sweet and aromatic with vanilla custard, rosehip, summer fruits, violet, sultana, cherry, moist sugar, and dark honey dribbling down over a toffee pudding; also some acacia notes.

Palate: A fragrant palate with touches of sandalwood and chocolate. Rich and broad in the middle (almost tarry), then dries nicely. Shows good grip and structure; rounded.

Finish: Fruit and oak.

Conclusion: More substantial and fruited than the Caribbean-aged rums of this age. Comes from a Coffey still.

Bristol Spirits, Long Pond 13yo

(Jamaica)

46% ABV

✪✪✪(✪)

Colour/Nose: A classic Wedderburn nose: punchy and pungent, with hints of banana skin, pineapple, wet grass, dunder. Sweet and sour. Water allows the fruit to develop.

Palate: Shows an oily feel with a tremendous spiky lift in the middle. Banana. Intense.

Finish: Light oak.

Conclusion: OK, so it's a love-or-hate thing (like peated malt) but if you want to understand rum, you must try this. You will learn to love it. A single-pot-still distillate.

Bristol Spirits, Long Pond 16yo

(oloroso cask finish; Jamaica)

46% ABV

✪✪✪(✪)

Colour/Nose: High-ester notes (plantain, grass, vegetation) calmed with notes of walnut, caramel.

Palate: Weighty but supple. Soft mid-palate, the more excessive notes in check. Sultana cake.

Finish: Oak.

Conclusion: Beginners start here.

Bristol Spirits, Monymusk 23yo

(Jamaica)

46% ABV

✪✪✪✪✪

Colour/Nose: Mature, slightly oaky, with notes of dried nuts and peels. Dried flowers. With water there's banana, powdered walnut, bitumen.

Palate: Broad, rich, vanilla, flambéed banana, baked fruits, and nuts. Superb structure.

Finish: Soft and long. Fruity.

Conclusion: Superb balance. Single-pot-still spirit.

Bristol Spirits, Monymusk 25yo

(Bourbon finish; Jamaica)

46% ABV

✪✪✪✪(✪)

Colour/Nose: Gold. Clean and quite nutty with notes of muscovado, chocolate, dried peels, vanilla, and fresh timber. Slightly lean but with almost smoky depths. Classic, mature.

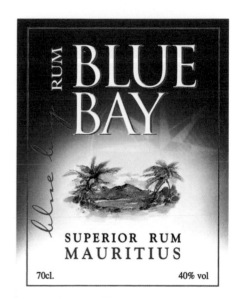

Palate: Dried fruits, nut, flowers, and allspice with a lift of maraschino cherry. Refined with coconut sweetness from the oak. Good balance.

Conclusion: An extremely classy, mature, spirit that's somehow similar to a lighter Speyside malt.

Bristol Spirits Port Morant 12yo
(Guyana)
46% ABV
✪✪✪✪

Colour/Nose: Demerara sugar, leather, spice. Oily/waxy and lightly vegetal, like jungle undergrowth. Funky, rich, and wonderful.

Palate: Nutty and crisp with a creamy nuttiness (Brazils). Central sweetness. Ripe mango.

Finish: Long and fruity.

Conclusion: A well-weighted, rich, single pot still.

Bristol Spirits Port Morant 20yo
(Limousin oak finish; Guyana)
46% ABV
✪✪✪✪

Colour/Nose: Vanilla spice and strangely exotic. Rosehips. Oak. Toast.

Palate: Rich and soft. Muscovado sugar with a lift of anise/fennel and ripe, tropical fruits. Perfumed oak. Exotic.

Finish: Long and oaky, with a hint of molasses.

Conclusion: Lovely balance.

Bristol Spirits, Providence Still 10yr
(Trinidad)
46% ABV
✪✪✪(✪)

Colour/Nose: Very pale. Charming, sweet, and soft with passion-fruit, cane juice, pineapple, barley sugar. Hint of smoky oak.

Palate: Sweet and quite concentrated, with balance between cinnamon, pecan pie, and peanut brittle. Velvety feel.

Finish: Rice Crispies.

Conclusion: As sweet as you'd expect from Trinidad but with extra depth. Coffey still spirit.

Bristol Spirits, Rockley Still 16yo
(Fino finish; Barbados)
46% ABV
✪✪✪✪

Colour/Nose: Pale gold. Pungent, almost smoky nose with a touch of wet grass and aromas of tahini/sesame and tarry ropes. Atypical Bajan. With water there's dried mango and caramelized fruit juice.

Palate: Beautifully rounded and subtle. Brown sugar with those burnt, fruit-syrup flavours. Ginger, charred apricot.

Conclusion: Shut your eyes and this could be an Islay malt finished in a rum cask.

Bristol Spirits Versailles 18yo
(port cask finish; Guyana)
46% ABV
✪✪✪(✪)

Colour/Nose: Hint of pink. Delicate and quite floral to start with, then dried fruits, herbs, sweet spices, and orange. Fairly firm oak. Port note.

Palate: Almost biscuity to start, then cashew, eucalyptus; softens into a rich, quite spicy, herbal mouthful.

Finish: Sloe.

Conclusion: Ripe and well-balanced. A double-pot-still spirit.

Bundaberg (Australia)
Owned by Diageo
Bundaberg, Queensland, Australia
From the cane fields of Queensland.
An iconic brand in Australia.
Tel: + 61 7 4150 2999/8684
Fax: + 61 7 4131 8966
Website: www.bundabergrum.com.au

Bundaberg
37% ABV
(✪)

Colour/Nose: Deep gold/orange. Raw spirit, apple. Hard and industrial.

Palate: Nutty, parma violet with a bitter edge.

Finish: Hot.

Conclusion: Unbalanced, raw, and nasty.

Bundaberg Black
40% ABV
(✪)

Colour/Nose: Red/amber. Dried-up wood.

Palate: Herbal, some wood, then raw spirit. Unbalanced.

Finish: Persistent (sadly).

Conclusion: Searing. No redeeming features.

Bundaberg O. P.

57.7% ABV

✿

Colour/Nose: Orange/amber. Nutty, apple core notes. Dry grass, broad-bean pods.

Palate: Strangely yeasty.

Finish: Hot.

Conclusion: The best of the bunch.

Wm. Cadenhead (UK)

Campbeltown, Scotland

This firm was established in Aberdeen in 1842 as a whisky and Demerara rum broker and has been bottling its own range of single-cask and blended rums ever since. Now part of the family firm that owns Springbank malt whisky distillery.

Tel: +44 (0) 1586 554258

Fax: +44 (0) 1586 551393

Email: enquiries@wmcadenhead.com

Website: www.wmcadenhead.com

Cadenhead's Barbados 15yo

46% ABV

✿✿✿✿

Colour/Nose: Pale gold. Slightly vegetal, intense, almost smoky nose with herbs, lilies, pollen. Water brings out an oily leather note, then beeswax.

Palate: Medium-bodied, with apple, raisin, and spices. A voluptuous mid-palate where all the sweetness lurks like honey on Greek yoghurt. Dry on the sides and back of the mouth.

Finish: Charred. A little short.

Conclusion: A love-it-or-hate-it rum. I love it!

Cadenhead's Demerara 10yo

46% ABV

✿✿✿

Colour/Nose: Very pale. Rich nose with mead, peach-stone, and some charred notes. Wood seems a little tired.

Palate: Fine and clean with acacia honey all the way. Light, flavour-wise, but a soft feel.

Finish: Slightly peppery. Short.

Conclusion: The colour infers little interaction between cask and spirit, borne out by the palate.

Cadenhead's Guyanan 13yo

46% ABV

✿✿(✿)

Colour/Nose: Very pale straw. Light, sweet, floral with notes of mandarin and banana. with With water: lightly oaky. Wood is dull again.

Palate: Medium- to full-bodied. A solid, mellow, mid-palate with hint of mango.

Finish: Dies quickly.

Conclusion: Again, fresher wood is needed.

Cadenhead's Jamaican 13yo

46% ABV

✿✿

Colour/Nose: Pale straw. Very light aroma of sweet, fresh fruit.

Palate: Coconut immediately and real spiciness from the cask, but little happening rum-wise.

Finish: Dry. Some oak.

Conclusion: Lacks that classic Jamaican punch and energy.

Cadenhead's Demerara 10yo

(Laphroaig cask finish)

46% ABV

✿

Colour/Nose: Very, very pale. Light notes of apple and raisin and some molasses/liquorice. In time, a "grainy", immature note.

Palate: Sweet centre with apricot, peach, and banana. Oily but no maturity.

Finish: Light smoke.

Conclusion: The cask seems dead. Finishing in a Laphroaig cask might be a better idea.

Cadenhead's Port Morant/Uitvlugt 30yo

(Guyana)

73.3% ABV

✿✿✿✿✿

Colour/Nose: Dark amber with reddish glints. Cask influence: perfumed notes on top; sweet spices, cocoa, rum truffles, cigar smoke, dried fruits, polished oak. Complex, elegant, mature.

Palate: Beautiful balanced: sweet and savoury, wood and spirit: roasted nuts, chocolate, honey.

Finish: Long, in fact everlasting.

Conclusion: A stunning old rum. Be careful: it's bloody strong!

Cadenhead's VNL/Enmore 30yo
(Guyana)
62.9% ABV
❍❍❍❍❍

Colour/Nose: Reddish amber. Deep, sweet, and concentrated; crème brûlée, caramelized fruits, fruit cake, toffee pudding. Sweet power.

Palate: Sweet and mouth-filling. Toffee, vanilla, big (balanced) oak. Sweet yet edgy, a glorious balance between spice and toffee.

Finish: Long.

Conclusion: This is a fantastic rum which hasn't been dominated by the cask.

Caney (Cuba)

Santiago de Cuba, Cuba
Tel: +53 22 2 5576

Ron Caney Añejo Centurio
38% ABV
❍❍

Colour/Nose: Brown. Quite a spirity hit. Dry and hard, reminiscent of dried orange peel.

Palate: Light and spicy with a touch of nutmeg and peanut brittle. Some slightly stale wood.

Finish: Hot.

Conclusion: Another Cuban brand that's only available on the domestic market.

Captain Morgan (International)

Owned by Diageo
Stamford, Connecticut, USA
London, UK
Created by Seagram in the late 1940s, this brand is now one of the biggest-selling rums in the world, with an ever-increasing portfolio, from a "British"-style blend to spiced and flavoured.
Tel: + 00 1 203 359 7100;
    +44 (0)20 7927 5200
Fax: + 00 1 203 967 7730;
    +44 (0)20 7927 4795
Website: www.rum.com

Captain Morgan
(Blend of Jamaican, Guyanese, Barbadian)
40% ABV
❍❍

Colour/Nose: Reddish amber. Toffee, raisin, caramel, tinned pineapple. Seems young.

Palate: Light and soft; treacle toffee softness in the centre.

Finish: Short and bitter.

Conclusion: Really not a lot going on in there.

Captain Morgan Private Stock
(Puerto Rico)
40% ABV
❍❍(❍)

Colour/Nose: Old gold. Vanilla and spice.

Palate: Perfumed palate with sweet cinnamon. Decent weight and delivery.

Finish: Spicy.

Conclusion: The higher alcohol seems to help.

Captain Morgan Original Spiced Rum
(Puerto Rico)
35% ABV
❍

Colour/Nose: Old gold. Light with a little prickle of vanilla and cinnamon stick.

Palate: Raw, thin, and hollow.

Finish: Spirity.

Conclusion: Very poor.

Captain Morgan Parrot Bay
(Coconut rum, Puerto Rico)
24% ABV
❍❍❍

Colour/Nose: Clear. Bright. Sweet cocoa butter.

Palate: Nutty and dry. The spirit seems a little raw and not quite knitted to the flavour.

Finish: Sugar.

Conclusion: Sticky and sweet.

Morgan's Spiced
(UK version)
37.5% ABV
❍❍

Colour/Nose: Very slick and sweet with loads of vanilla, coconut, and ginger.

Palate: Soft and quite gentle with little jabs
of spiciness over almost chocolatey creaminess.
Finish: Sweet.
Conclusion: More citrus and vanilla than spiced.

Caribbean Club (Cuba)

Distributed by Cimez
Tel: + 53 7 204 2126/204 0774
Fax: + 53 7 204 1996
E-mail: elastra@cimex.com.cu

Caribbean Club Añejo 7 Años

38% ABV

OO

Colour/Nose: Amber/mahogany. Light and
a little slick: tangerine, pecan. Water brings
out marzipan/almond paste and a touch
of spirit.
Palate: Slightly hollow but there's spiciness,
baked apple, and orange peel around it,
along with milk chocolate.
Finish: Short. Wood.
Conclusion: Another domestic Cuban brand.
Doesn't quite deliver. The wood is a little dull.

Caroni (Trinidad)

The rum division of the government-
controlled sugar industry. Rum Distillers
of Trinidad & Tobago Caroni (1975) has
been distilling and blending rums since
1918. A major bulk exporter, it holds
the largest stock of aged column- and
pot-still rums on the island.
Tel: +868 662 3645
Fax: + 868 663 1404
Website: www.trinidadrum.com

Caroni Superb White Magic 7yo

43% ABV

OOO

Colour/Nose: Clear, bright. Good direct
impact with some creamy richness; a hint
of molasses.
Palate: Soft. All in the middle of the mouth.
Clean.
Finish: Tingling, fresh, and crisp.
Conclusion: Well-made. A mixer.

Caroni Felicite 4yo

43% ABV

OOO

Colour/Nose: Straw. Light, with a banana hint.
Palate: Sweet and gently spicy. Pleasant feel.
Finish: Short.
Conclusion: The lightest of this firm's aged rums.

Caroni Old Cask 10yo

43% ABV

OOOO

Colour/Nose: Complexity built into a light
frame: vanilla, lemon, nutmeg, lots of coconut.
Palate: Quite dry with light tannins, white
chocolate, and soft fruit. Retains a crisp feel.
Finish: Clean.
Conclusion: Caroni has huge potential and
great stocks and here's evidence of that.

Caroni Legend 2000 Gold 15yo

43% ABV

OOO(O)

Colour/Nose: Golden. Vanilla and passion-fruit.
Palate: Clean with good (light to medium-
bodied) weight and drive, with good energy in
the mouth. Coconut and mango. Very clean.
Finish: Clean.
Conclusion: Good balance of sweet and spicy.

Caroni Stallion Puncheon (White overproof)

75% ABV

OOO(O)

Colour/Nose: Clear, bright. High-toned and
intense: lemon, lime, banana peel.
Palate: Rich feel with some green chilli and fruit.
Finish: Vapourizes.
Conclusion: This and Caroni Velvet Smooth
Overproof (also 75%) are, the firm assures
me, the same product. Both are powerful,
assertive beasts.

Chairman's Reserve (St Lucia)

Owned by St Lucia Distillers
Castries, St Lucia
One of the most innovative rum-makers
in the Caribbean, with a portfolio
targeting (and creating) every possible
niche in an expanding market. With

columns and two types of pot stills, it appears to have all the bases covered.
Tel: +758 451 4258
Fax: +758 451 4221
Email: info@sludistillers.com
Website: www.sludistillers.com

Chairman's Reserve

40% ABV

✪✪✪✪(✪)

Colour/Nose: Pot-still richness: juicy fruits, tanned leather with dried fruits and honey on top.
Palate: Medium-bodied with soft feel. Spice, vanilla, banana. An almost earthy undertow.
Finish: Soft.
Conclusion: A very stylish rum. Shows skilful blending.

Clarke's Court (Grenada)

Owned by Grenada Sugar Factory
St George's, Grenada
Founded in 1937, Grenada Sugar Factory is the largest of this spice island's distillers and its overproof white the biggest seller on the island.
Tel: + 473 444 5363/576 3876
Fax: +473 444 24652
Website: www.clarkescourtrum.com

Clarke's Court Light Rum

40% ABV

✪✪(✪)

Colour/Nose: Light citric (tangerine) alongside peanut notes. Full-flavoured and quite sweet.
Palate: Thick. Shows good weight with ripe, lemon-lime peel, and that peanut again; begins to dry towards the finish. Assertive neat, but water makes it a little flat and dull.
Finish: Dry. Light banana.
Conclusion: Bigger than most "light" rums.

Clarke's Court Pure White Rum

69% ABV

✪✪✪

Colour/Nose: Pungent, almost phenolic. Peanuts appear again, and oil with a slight rubbery note. Powerful.

Palate: Sweet start and oily feel. Dilute, and it becomes quite vegetal.
Finish: Dry.
Conclusion: A strong, rich, oily overproof.

Clarke's Court Dark

43% ABV

✪✪✪(✪)

Colour/Nose: Gold. Light to medium-bodied, with hints of dried guava, banana, and some orange. Attractive with soft weight and vanilla/coconut wood notes.
Palate: Sweet, medium-bodied, and syrupy on the mid-palate, with some papaya freshened up by biscuity wood.
Finish: Coconut.
Conclusion: Good balance between a sweet spirit and clean, crisp oak. Well-made.

Clarke's Court Lemon

35% ABV

✪✪✪

Colour/Nose: Clear, bright. Full with a lime leaf and oil note.
Palate: Sticky and sweet with a thick feel. Lime and coconut. Rounded.
Finish: Coconut.
Conclusion: The sweetest lime in the bunch. No need for sugar if you're making a daiquiri with this!

Clément (Martinique)

Le François, Martinique
Homère Clément is considered as the father of *rhum agricole*. Today his estate with its elegant gardens, (silent) distillery, and typical planter's house is a tourist attraction. The rums are made at Simon.
Tel: + 596 596 54 62 07
Fax: + 596 596 54 63 50
Email: communication.clement@gbh.fr
Website: www.rhum-clement.com

Clément Blanc

50% ABV

✪✪✪

Colour/Nose: Light, nutty, and pungent. Full-flavoured with notes of violet. Oily.

Palate: Rich, sweet, and ripe. Rounded texture.

Finish: Firm.

Conclusion: A powerful, assertive example.

Clément Grappe Blanche

50% ABV

○○○○

Colour/Nose: Lighter with more notes of wild flower, liquorice, and anise.

Palate: Soft, very gentle, clean, and elegant.

Finish: Soft.

Conclusion: Clément's premium white rum.

Clément Canne Bleu

50% ABV

○○○(○)

Colour/Nose: Fruity, ripe, sweet, and direct. Melon and mango. A touch of grass.

Palate: Clean. Limey, crisp. Good, soft weight.

Finish: Clean. Dry.

Conclusion: Rum from a single cane species.

Clément Vieux

50% ABV

○○○○

Colour/Nose: Amber. Lemon/acacia. Almost like a rye whiskey. Sweet and elegant with tingling notes of resin and sap. Well-integrated.

Palate: Spicy yet gentle. Well-balanced.

Finish: Long.

Conclusion: Extremely well put together.

Clément Cuvée Charles

○○○(○)

Colour/Nose: Amber. Resinous note. Clean and quite oily. Syrupy fruits, almost honeyed. Powerful.

Palate: Crème brûlée, floral spiciness. Supple.

Finish: Complex.

Conclusion: A nice blend of three- and six-year-old rums.

Clément Cuvée Homère

○○○○

Colour/Nose: Dark amber. Richer, more complex than the Charles. Dried nuts and fruits.

Palate: Wood shows in a spicy manner but the sweet fruit hold things together. Caramelized fruits and oak. Grippy.

Finish: Dry.

Conclusion: A six-year-old rum. More austere but will appeal to classicists.

Clément XO

○○○(○)

Colour/Nose: Amber. Gentle and sweeter with dried apricot, toffee apple, and banana notes.

Palate: Sultana, treacle; develops cognac-like flavours of nuts and fruits. Tight with firm grip.

Finish: Nutty.

Conclusion: Firm but fine.

Clément 10yo

○○○(○)

Colour/Nose: Sandalwood, dried roses, acacia, and very light toffee. Quite austere.

Palate: Richer than the nose suggests, with a spicy feel along with the scented wood.

Finish: Dry.

Conclusion: In a similar vein to the XO.

Clément 1976

○○○○

Colour/Nose: Copper. Fragrant: eucalyptus, rose, even some perfumed lily and rose.

Palate: Dry and clean with some ashy wood and fine floral notes. Clean with good grip.

Finish: Dry.

Conclusion: Classic dry, restrained Clément style.

Clément 1952

○○○○

Colour/Nose: Vanilla, smoke, and ripe toffee.

Palate: Soft, gentle, and elegant the taste of leather alongside faded flowers, honey, spice.

Finish: Oak.

Conclusion: Perfumed and sultry.

Cockspur (Barbados)

Owned by Hanschell Innis

Brighton, St Michael, Barbados

The brand name of one of Barbados' oldest bottlers, Hanschell Innis (est. 1884). The rums are made at the West Indies Rum Distillery.

Tel: +809 425 9393

Fax: +809 425 8371

Email: hanschell@goddent.com

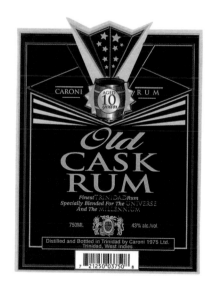

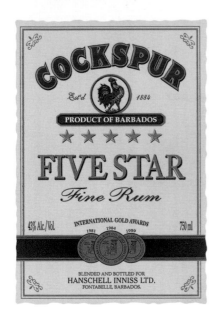

Cockspur Five Star

40% ABV

✪✪✪✪

Colour/Nose: Light amber. Vanilla with a touch of nutmeg. Attractively gentle; gets creamier, opening into black-cherry cheesecake and mango.

Palate: Good balance between soft, honeyed centre and ginger. Some lemon and kumquat.

Finish: Gingery.

Conclusion: Lovely balance.

Cockspur Old Gold

40% ABV

✪✪✪(✪)

Colour/Nose: Clean with some mature, oaky notes. Baked apple, pear, fruitcake.

Palate: Charcoal on top of mellow, ripe fruit.

Finish: Oak.

Conclusion: Older, more mature. Slightly oaky.

Cockspur VSOR

43% ABV

✪✪✪✪

Colour/Nose: Lifted and aromatic: dried rose, pot pourri, menthol, violet. Also spice: coriander, black pepper on strawberry and dried fruits.

Palate: Sweet and soft. Very spicy and quite weighty. Some orange, black banana and toffee.

Finish: Rich.

Conclusion: Reminds me of old leather armchairs.

Cruzan (US Virgin Islands)

Part of the C.L. Global Brands Group St Croix, US Virgin Islands

The Nelthropp family has been distilling in St Croix for seven generations, and today the distillery (now part of the C.L./ Angostura empire) is one of the most modern in the Caribbean. All of the rums are aged for a minimum of two years.

Tel: + 1 561 837 6300
Fax: + 1 561 832 4556
Website: www.cruzanrum.com

Cruzan Estate Light Rum 2yo

40% ABV

✪✪(✪)

Colour/Nose: Clear, bright. Light with the merest hint of nut and daffodil. Touch of citrus fruit.

Palate: Good weight and creamy feel. Clean.

Finish: Short and fresh.

Conclusion: Well-made. Will act as a fine base for cocktails.

Cruzan Clipper 2yo

(Spiced rum)

60% ABV

✪✪✪

Colour/Nose: Orangey-gold. Citric: dried orange peel, tangerine marmalade, along with balanced American oak notes: vanilla, toast, and honey; ginger. Clean and precise.

Palate: Sweet and light in body, but with a delicious spiciness and a lick of orange butter.

Finish: Toasty with mandarin. Tingly.

Conclusion: Very well-made and attractive.

Cruzan Estate Dark 2yo

40% ABV

✪✪✪(✪)

Colour/Nose: Clear, bright. Filled with fruits: baked apple, passion-fruit, mango, and an intense juicy note akin to orange Curaçao. Light touch of allspice.

Palate: Soft, smooth, and gentle with finely balanced oak.

Finish: Toasty.

Conclusion: Clean and high-toned. Great handling of spirit and wood.

Cruzan Estate Diamond 5yo

40% ABV

✪✪✪✪

Colour/Nose: Glowing amber. Most substantial of range with Bourbon-like character: signature orange, with cinnamon, honeysuckle blossom.

Palate: Balance struck between clean oak and sweet spirit: macadamia nut, coconut, vanilla, honey, banana. Fine, dusty feel.

Finish: Soft and sweet.

Conclusion: Stylish and structured. Impressive work done here with wood management.

Cruzan Single Barrel

40% ABV

✪✪✪✪(✪)

Colour/Nose: Light amber. Spiciest of the range, also the most complex.Subtle notes of marzipan, chestnut purée, mint, barley-sugar, orange pekoe tea, light chamois leather.
Palate: Sweet and ripe with papaya, galia melon, banana. Lovely weight on the middle.
Finish: Fresh and dry.
Conclusion: Develops beautifully in the glass. Give this plenty of time. Fine, light, and elegant.

Cruzan Banana
27.5% ABV
✪✪(✪)
Colour/Nose: Clear and bright. Dried banana chips with a hint of unripe banana.
Palate: Sweet and slightly spicy. Better than the nose, though more artificial than much of the rest of the range.
Finish: Fruity.
Conclusion: Not the most convincing, but still good in mixed drinks.

Cruzan Coconut
27.5% ABV
✪✪✪
Colour/Nose: Clear, bright. Light and clean. Moist, desiccated coconut with a slightly green note. The freshest of the coconut rums.
Palate: Creamy with good, natural-seeming flavours. Maybe just lacks some weight.
Finish: Clean, if a bit short.
Conclusion: Will pep up a cocktail.

Cruzan Mango
27.5% ABV
✪✪✪(✪)
Colour/Nose: Clear, bright. Sweet but juicy with mango flesh along with sugar syrup.
Palate: Fruity with light vanilla notes.
Finish: Clean.
Conclusion: Attractive. Great in a rum punch.

Cruzan Orange
27.5% ABV
✪✪✪
Colour/Nose: Clear, bright. Sweet orange/tangerine zest – very zesty. Clean.
Palate: Tangerine sweetness. Smooth and soft; tingling mid-palate. Sweetens towards the end.

Finish: Sweet, slightly sugary.
Conclusion: Well-made and attractive.

Cruzan Pineapple
27.5% ABV
✪✪✪✪
Colour/Nose: Clear, bright. Tinned pineapple and fresh pineapple juice. Fresh and clean.
Palate: Lighter in weight than the rest; also the juiciest in the stable. Clean, very good.
Finish: Fresh and quite dry.
Conclusion: The lighter weight allows the flavours to show well.

Cruzan Vanilla
27.5% ABV
✪✪✪(✪)
Colour/Nose: Clear and bright. Full and heavy vanilla tones, almost like a vanilla milk shake.
Palate: Soft and gentle. An attractive tingle in the middle prevents it becoming too cloying
Finish: Coconut.
Conclusion: Thick but clean.

Crystal (St Lucia)
Owned by St Lucia Distillers
Castries, St Lucia
Tel: +758 451 4258
Fax: +758 451 4221
Email: info@sludistillers.com
Website: www.sludistillers.com

Crystal White Rum
40% ABV
✪✪✪
Colour/Nose: Clear, bright. Light and dry with vanilla, fruit, and lime. Decent concentration.
Palate: Clean and very dry. Bone-dry, in fact.
Finish: Crisp.
Conclusion: Another good light rum. Very efficiently made.

Crystal Lime
35% ABV
✪✪✪(✪)
Colour/Nose: Very limey. zest and juice.
Palate: Very zesty to start. Sweet with an oily, soft feel. Great zingy drive.

Finish: Fresh.

Conclusion: Well-made. One of the better citrus fruit-flavoured rums.

Denro's (St Lucia)
Owned by St Lucia Distillers

Denro's Strong

(White overproof)

70% ABV

❁❁❁

Colour/Nose: Banana and red fruits (raspberries) drive nose. Slight metallic hint.

Palate: Soft and sweet, with hints of anise.

Finish: Dry.

Conclusion: Big and powerful. Try this in raspberry mint daiquiri!

Depaz (Martinique)
Part of the Bardinet/
La Martiniquaise group
St-Pierre, Martinique

Depaz is the only distillery remaining in St-Pierre, the northern town which was destroyed in the eruption of Mont Pelée in 1902.

Tel: +595 596 78 13 14

Fax: +596 596 78 30 28

Email: depazdist@hotmail.com

Website: www.depaz.fr

Depaz Blanc

50% ABV

❁❁(❁)

Colour/Nose: Clear, bright. Slightly earthy nose with soft fruits behind. More tropical with water.

Palate: Tight, with kiwi fruit, lychee, and pear.

Finish: Clean.

Conclusion: Quite light and delicate.

Depaz Vieux

45% ABV

❁❁❁(❁)

Colour/Nose: Light amber. Lots of apple and dry grass and a hint of cane. Complex. Some black pepper, paprika, and oak.

Palate: Fine, delicate, and crisp.

Finish: This is where the soft sugar still lurks.

Conclusion: Very good balance.

Dillon (Martinique)
Part of the Bardinet/La
Martiniquaise group
Fort-de-France, Martinique

Dillon's Fort de France distillery first started making *rhum agricole* in 1954. It is now one of the best-known of the brands in the export markets.

Tel: + 596 596 75 20 20

Fax: +596 596 75 30 33

Email: dgr.dillon@sasi.fr

Website: www.rhum-dillon.com

Dillon Blanc

50% ABV

❁(❁)

Colour/Nose: Pungent and slightly estery. Cooked banana, tinned pears. A little hard.

Palate: Dry and clean but, again, hard.

Finish: Firm.

Conclusion: Average.

Dillon Vieux

50% ABV

❁❁

Colour/Nose: Gold/amber. Some spice, lemon.

Palate: A little flat and lacking in life.

Finish: Slightly dry.

Conclusion: Average.

Dillon Hors d'Age XO

43% ABV

❁(❁)

Colour/Nose: Amber. Lean and angular.

Palate: Hard, seems forced.

Finish: Crisp.

Conclusion: Not for me.

Don Q (Puerto Rico)
Mercedita, Puerto Rico
Owned by Destilería Serrallès

Founded in 1865 in the city of Ponce. Still family owned, the firm's rums remain Puerto Rican's favourite brands.

Tel: + 1 797 840 1000

Fax: + 1 797 840 1155

Website: www.donqrum.com

Don Q Cristal

40% ABV

✪✪✪(✪)

Colour/Nose: Clear, bright. Clean with light citrus fruits and vanilla Soft and sweet.

Palate: Lots of vanilla richness giving good weight to the palate. Hint of molasses, lemon and light nutmeg/ginger. Clean.

Finish: Refreshing.

Conclusion: Very well-made, stylish white rum.

Don Q Gold

40% ABV

✪✪✪(✪)

Colour/Nose: Gold. Clean with more tropical fruit than the silver and a touch of coconut.

Palate: Guava and papaya mixed with light, sweet spice and a crisp, tobacco edge. Clean.

Finish: Lightly fruity

Conclusion: Very well-made.

Don Q Añejo

40% ABV

✪✪✪✪

Colour/Nose: Old gold. Oak-derived aromas and more weight. Red plum, cranberry juiciness.

Palate: A complex blend of chocolate, spice, sweet tobacco, and smooth vanilla sweetness.

Finish: Fruit and spicy oak.

Conclusion: Very classy blend.

Don Q Grand Añejo

40% ABV

✪✪✪✪(✪)

Colour/Nose: Old gold. Sweet and spicy with polished oak, orange peel, liquorice, nuts. Though dry, not overly woody. Complex.

Palate: Sweet and soft with mini explosions of flavour: orange toffee, coconut, dried fruits.

Finish: Light, charred oak.

Conclusion: First produced in 1993 to celebrate Puerto Rico's 500th anniversary. A blend of rums of up to twelve years of age. Very well-made.

Doorly's (Barbados)

Owned by R. L. Seale

Foursquare Distillery,

St Phillip, Barbados

Another old Barbadian bottler's brand which has been bought by R. L. Seale.

Tel: + 1 246 426 0334

Fax: + 1 246 436 6003

E-mail: rumfactory@sunbeach.net

Website: www.foursquarerum.com

Doorly's 5yo

40% ABV

✪✪✪

Colour/Nose: Gold. Light, sweet nose. Lightly fragrant: passion-fruit, papaya, vanilla custard, then in time, old-fashioned ginger beer.

Palate: Soft and gentle. Lovely balance of wood and soft spirit. Good weight.

Finish: Clean, easygoing, sweet.

Conclusion: A light, straightforward style.

Doorly's XO (Barbados)

40% ABV

✪✪✪✪✪

Colour/Nose: Medium-weight and elegant. Some nuttiness, then rich, perfumed sweetness: acacia honey, mango. Full, complex, and sweet.

Palate: A subtle, vanilla-laden complexity. Baked banana, sweet raisin, sultana, hint of walnut. Soft and elegant. Great balance.

Finish: Long and sweet. Tangerine.

Conclusion: Has spent a short time finishing in ex-sherry casks – rounds and gives another layer of flavour without dominating. Sip on its own.

El Dorado (Guyana)

Owned by Demerara Distillers

Georgetown, Guyana

The brand name of Demerara Distillers, a firm that not only has a remarkable collection of stills – allowing them to employ a huge range of marks in their blends – but is at the forefront of building Caribbean-owned international brands.

Tel: + 592 265 6000

Fax: + 592 265 3367

Website: www.demrum.com

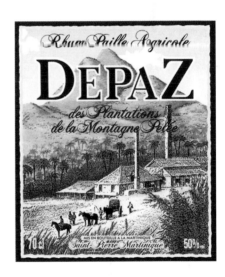

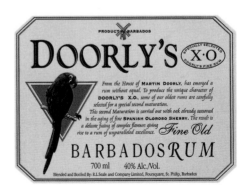

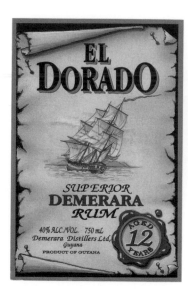

El Dorado White
37.5% ABV

✪✪✪(✪)

Colour/Nose: Rich and sweet. Banana, vanilla, and a mandarin-like citrus character.
Palate: Soft and gentle with silky weight.
Finish: Clean and sweet.
Conclusion: Decent body and weight. Cocktails.

El Dorado Gold
37.5% ABV

✪✪(✪)

Colour/Nose: Gold. Sweet. Overripe banana, honeysuckle, molasses. Creamy and thick.
Palate: Sweet and syrupy. Medium-bodied.
Finish: Sweet.
Conclusion: Perfectly decent.

El Dorado Dark
37.5% ABV

✪✪(✪)

Colour/Nose: Dark. More treacle toffee and a touch more weight. Banana loaf, chocolate.
Palate: Clean, soft, molasses, and date.
Finish: Soft.
Conclusion: Not too confected. Well-made.

El Dorado 5yo
40% ABV

✪✪✪✪

Colour/Nose: Amber. Clean and delicious.
Palate: Better weight; an added degree of complexity but still a medium-bodied rum. Very mellow with a chewy quality. Ripe fruits.
Finish: Soft and gentle.
Conclusion: Hugely, dangerously, drinkable.

El Dorado 12yo
40% ABV

✪✪✪✪✪

Colour/Nose: Rich gold/amber. Complex with sweet weight, but not OTT. Balanced, spicy oak and layers of elegant, ripe fruits.
Palate: Mouth-coating and soft. Light nutmeg character with rich resonant notes of chestnut, toffee, latté, and baked banana, with a citric lift.
Finish: Nutmeg and spice.
Conclusion: If anything, as good as the 15yo.

El Dorado 15yo
40% ABV

✪✪✪✪✪

Colour/Nose: Mahogany. Big, deep, and complex. Soft sugars, coffee, caramelized fruits.
Palate: An extra dimension, with more oak. Rich, heavy spirit in the blend giving weight; the oak adding structure and some lighter, citric notes provide complexity.
Finish: Long and complex.
Conclusion: These classic Demerara rums don't get fat and oaky, but build in complexity and weight. A classic.

El Dorado 21yo Special Reserve
43% ABV

✪✪✪✪

Colour/Nose: Reddish amber. Driest of the range with more wood: cigar box, walnut. Some earthy notes along with fig and sweet honey.
Palate: As silky as ever, this time with acacia.
Finish: Bitter orange-peel, pecan.
Conclusion: Twenty-one and still going strong. That's evidence of a rich base spirit and clever wood management.

El Dorado Spiced Rum
40% ABV

✪✪✪(✪)

Colour/Nose: Gold. Notes of cinnamon, ginger, and lots of nutmeg; almost makes you sneeze. With water, turns to light clove and allspice. Suitably exotic.
Palate: A mélange of spices over quite light spirit. Clean, light, and rather lovely.
Finish: Sweet and spicy.
Conclusion: Natural and well-made.

English Harbour
Owned by Antigua Distillery
St John's, Antigua
The export brand of Antigua Distillers (est. 1932). The local brands are sold under the Cavalier label.
Tel: + 268 462 1072
Fax: + 268 460 4266
Website: www.antiguadistillery.com

English Harbour White 3yo

40% ABV

ooo

Colour/Nose: Clear, bright. Lime-zest notes blend with almonds and peanuts, and with water, there's an attractive green vegetal note. Clean.
Palate: Sweet and clean with kumquat and a light, earthy touch adding interest. Oily feel.
Finish: Clean and decent.
Conclusion: A white rum with good weight and sweet flavours.

English Harbour Golden 3yo

40% ABV

ooo(o)

Colour/Nose: Gold to amber. Spicy, earthy notes mix with peanut biscuits alongside soft caramel and a lift from touches of apple sauce and lime.
Palate: Plenty of spicy oak balancing a chewy texture which has light, banana toffee hints.
Finish: Nutty.
Conclusion: A quite stylish, medium-bodied rum. Well made.

English Harbour Extra Old

40% ABV

oooo(o)

Colour/Nose: Copper/amber with a green glint. Weighty, mature nose (oak, warehouses, walnuts) alongside coconut husk, dry nuts, and dried peels, overripe banana, black fruits. Smooth.
Palate: Oaky but balanced and chewy. Medium-bodied. Dry tea leaves, spice, tobacco and lovely layers of fruit. Fungal notes.
Finish: Dry.
Conclusion: Mature and elegant. Great, naturally aged rum. Recommended.

51 Cachaça (Brazil)

Owned by Industrías Muller de Bebidas, São Paulo, Brazil
This cachaça claims to be the second-largest-selling spirit brand in the world, selling over twenty million cases a year, mostly in Brazil.
Tel: + 55 195 61 5151
Fax: + 55 195 61 5522

51 Cachaça

40% ABV

ooo(o)

Colour/Nose: Clear, bright. Lightly oily. Very clean with hints of lemon. Verging on neutral.
Palate: Sweet and slightly sugary with hint of children's sweeties. Whistle-clean.
Finish: Clean, light.
Conclusion: None of the vegetal notes usually associated with cachaça. Good, clean, light spirit.

La Favorite (Martinique)

Fort de France, Martinique
The Dormoy family has produced *rhum agricole* on this estate since 1909. One of the island's few independent producers.
Tel: + 596 596 50 47 32
Fax: + 596 596 50 49 84

La Favorite Vieux

50% ABV

ooo

Colour/Nose: Gold. Creamy, herbal, tangerines.
Palate: Soft, clean; good grip. Caramelized peach.
Finish: Dry and nutty.
Conclusion: Fair.

Ferdi's (Trinidad)

Part of C.L. Global Brands
Port of Spain, Trinidad & Tobago
Jo Fernandes started blending and distilling in the 1920s. He sold the firm and the brands to Angostura in 1973.
Tel: +868 623 1841/5
Fax: +868 623 1847
Email: icss@angostura.com
Website: www.angostura.com

Ferdi's

40% ABV

ooo(o)

Colour/Nose: Creamy vanillin; butterscotch, more generous, Trinidad-style, orange-tangerine.
Palate: Drier than nose suggests; wood in balance, some tangerine crème brûlée.
Finish: Clean and dry.
Conclusion: Great cocktail brand.

Fernandes (Trinidad)
Part of C.L. Global Brands
Port of Spain, Trinidad & Tobago
Tel: +868 623 1841/5
Fax: +868 623 1847
Email: icss@angostura.com
Website: www.angostura.com

Fernandes Black Label
40% ABV
✪✪✪

Colour/Nose: Gold. Fine weight with good solidity, some guava, mango notes. Lime zest.
Palate: The extra weight helps the mid-palate feel. Ginger, nutmeg.
Finish: Clean and dry.
Conclusion: A big-seller in Trinidad. Great mixer.

Flor de Caña (Nicaragua)
Owned by Compañía Licorera de Nicaragua, Managua, Nicaragua
This enterprising distiller has been producing aged brands at its distillery in Chichigalpa since 1937.
Tel: +505 278 3270/72
Fax: +505 277 3649
Website: www.flordecana.com

Flor de Caña Extra Dry 4yo
40% ABV
✪✪✪✪

Colour/Nose: Clean, bright. Mandarins, sweet, clean, and attractive with vanilla, light wood.
Palate: Crisp with good weight.
Finish: Clean.
Conclusion: A very good white rum.

Flor de Caña Black Label 5yo
40% ABV
✪✪✪✪

Colour/Nose: Amber. Bigger and richer. Apricot, green mango. Good balance between sweetness and oak.
Palate: Soft start and a creamy centre, with baked banana and tropical fruit balanced by roasted hazelnut.
Finish: Nutty.
Conclusion: Great balance, great style.

Flor de Caña Grand Reserve 7yo
40% ABV
✪✪✪✪(✪)

Colour/Nose: Amber. Similar to the Black label but richer and more complex. Cocoa, maple syrup, raspberry/strawberry, guava/passion-fruit, and complex oak notes.
Palate: Rich and sweet: black banana, fig, rich fruits but with a balanced, oaky character.
Finish: Long. Oaky.
Conclusion: A very classy rum from a very classy producer.

Flor de Caña Centenario 12 Años
40% ABV
✪✪✪(✪)

Colour/Nose: Reddish amber. More obvious wood, moving into nuts, mulch, redwood forest.
Palate: Mature and rich. Treacle in the mid-palate. Good weight, but a little tannic.
Finish: Firm. Oaky.
Conclusion: Begs for a cigar. A little on the woody side.

Foursquare Spiced (Barbados)
Owned by R. L. Seale
Foursquare Distillery, St Phillip, Barbados
Another brand from the ever fertile mind of Richard Seale, this one named after his ultra-modern distillery built on the site of the oldest Bajan sugar plantation.
Tel: + 1 246 426 0334
Fax: + 1 246 436 6003
E-mail: rumfactory@sunbeach.net
Website: www.foursquarerum.com

Foursquare Spiced
35% ABV
✪✪✪✪✪

Colour/Nose: Amber. Immediate hit of exotic spice: allspice, menthol, clove, nutmeg, ginger, then bitter orange and dried herbs.
Palate: Intense, perfumed, and quite dry. Great balance between bitter/sweet spices and herbs.
Finish: Gingery.
Conclusion: In a different league to other spiced rums. Simply sensational.

Germana (Brazil)

Nova Uniao, Minas Gerais, Brazil

The Caetano family's distillery in Minas Gerais has been making cachaça for over ninety years. They use a cane juice/maize starter, age in small oak barrels, and pack them in banana leaf-covered bottles.

Tel/Fax: + 55 55 31 3685 1256

Sales: +55 31 9973 3178

Germana Cachaça

41.6% ABV

✪✪✪✪(✪)

Colour/Nose: Light straw. Rich, sweet, lightly vegetal nose that mixes sweet and savoury notes: fresh sugar cane juice, banana, tomato leaf,

Palate: Wonderfully exotic. The cedary wood gives good structure for the banana notes.

Finish: Dry.

Conclusion: Classic, traditional cachaça. The best of its kind.

Gosling's (Bermuda)

Hamilton, Bermuda

Founded by James Gosling, a wine and spirit merchant originally from England, the firm has been blending rums since the mid-nineteenth century. The original Black Seal was a barrel proof rum sold in Champagne bottles that were sealed with black wax.

Tel: + 441 295 1123

Fax: + 441 292 1775

Email: cgosling@goslings.com

Website: www.blackseal.com

Gosling's Black Seal

(Bermuda/Caribbean blend)

40% ABV

✪✪✪(✪)

Colour/Nose: Red/mahogany. Stewed fruits, coffee, plum crumble, light treacle, and strangely, a touch of tomato. Cumin, asafoetida.

Palate: Soft, broad, and gentle with rich, sweet, black fruits.

Finish: Spicy, clean.

Conclusion: Well-blended and not at all forced.

Gosling's Black Seal 151 Proof

75% ABV

✪✪✪(✪)

Colour/Nose: Red/mahogany. A big blast of rumbustious alcohol along with caramel, lime.

Palate: Rich and fruity. Powerful. Molasses, plums slightly fragrant and spicy. Fizzes across the palate.

Finish: Medium length; spicy.

Conclusion: Not for the fainthearted.

Havana Club (Cuba)

Joint venture between the Cuban Government and Pernod-Ricard

La Havana, Cuba

The original Havana Club was first made in 1878. These days it's Cuba's best-known and most highly respected rum brand. Thanks to the joint venture it became the fastest-growing spirits brand in the world – which doesn't please Bacardi!

Tel: + 53 7 62 4108/61 8051

Fax: + 53 7 62 1825

E-mail: fundacionhc@ip.etecsa.cu

Website: www.havana-club.com

Havana Club Silver Dry

40% ABV

✪✪(✪)

Colour/Nose: Bright. Fresh and sweet with citric notes.

Palate: Soft and crisp, then as the citrus fruit appears, it softens and sweetens.

Finish: Crisp, soft if a little short.

Conclusion: A clean, straightforward mixing rum.

Havana Club Añejo Blanca

40% ABV

✪✪✪

Colour/Nose: Pale straw. Vegetal/leafy notes hint of honey.

Palate: Clean and soft with some nuttiness. Good feel with good weight and a touch of vanilla.

Finish: Soft and clean.

Conclusion: Brought in to replace Silver Dry, this has more weight and character.

Finish: Crisp and oaky.

Conclusion: Both of these are well-made, characterful spirits and are a welcome addition to the wide, weird world of rum.

Koko-Nut (St Lucia)

Owned by St Lucia Distillers
Castries, St Lucia
Tel: +758 451 4258
Fax: +758 451 4221
Email: info@sludistillers.com
Website: www.sludistillers.com

Koko-Nut

25% ABV
✪✪✪(✪)

Colour/Nose: Clear, bright. Leaner and clean with coconut milk and flesh.

Palate: Medium-sweet. Delivers real, full, coconut flavours. Sweet but not claggy.

Finish: Gentle.

Conclusion: The best-balanced coconut rum.

Kwèyòl (St Lucia)

Owned by St Lucia Distillers
Castries, St Lucia
Tel: +758 451 4258
Fax: +758 451 4221
Email: info@sludistillers.com
Website: www.sludistillers.com

Kwèyòl Spiced Rum

40% ABV
✪✪✪✪

Colour/Nose: Tremendous sweet spices on the nose: vanilla, allspice, nutmeg, Christmas cake.

Palate: Explosive entry which fills the mouth with sweet and tingling spices.

Finish: Clean, gingery.

Conclusion: One of the best spiced rums.

Lamb's (UK)

Owned by Allied-Domecq
London, England
Alfred Lamb was one of London's most famous rum brokers who started blending

in 1849. The company merged with two other firms to form United Rum Merchants after its premises were bombed in WWII. U.R.M. is now part of Allied-Domecq.
Tel: +44 (0) 20 7323 9000
Email: www.allieddomecqplc.com
Website: www.allieddomecqplc.com

Lamb's Navy Rum

40% ABV
✪✪✪(✪)

Colour/Nose: Reddish brown. Clean nose with touches of treacle, blackfruit pastille, demerara sugar. Not as confected as some. Young.

Palate: Clean with a little (Jamaican?) lift in the middle of the palate. Smooth. Fried plantain, nuts.

Finish: Dry and spicy.

Conclusion: The best of the old British style.

Lemon Hart (UK)

Owned by Allied-Domecq
London, England
Lemuel (Lemon) Hart was a nineteenth-century rum broker based in Cornwall who created this Jamaican blend in 1804.
Tel: +44 (0) 20 7323 9000
Email: www.allieddomecqplc.com
Website: www.allieddomecqplc.com

Lemon Hart Jamaican Rum

40% ABV
✪✪✪(✪)

Colour/Nose: Light amber. Banana split with touch of molasses and good lift from pineappley esters. Water brings out orange peel and lemon.

Palate: Good weight; medium-rich mid-palate. Soft with musky orange, pineapple, and banana.

Finish: Fresh. Touch of oak.

Conclusion: Very approachable, mixable, well-blended rum.

Malibu (UK)

Owned by Allied-Domecq
London, UK
The brand that brought more new drinkers into the category than any other.

It uses Barbadian spirit from W.I.R.D. but is blended in Scotland.
Tel: +44 (0) 20 7323 9000
Email: www.allieddomecqplc.com
Website: www.allieddomecqplc.com

Malibu Coconut
21% ABV
✪✪✪
Colour/Nose: Clear; bright. Sweet with vanilla and tinned coconut milk. Light but fresh.
Palate: Light and medium-sweet. Decent sweet coconut flavours. Slightly thin on the palate.
Finish: Sugary.
Conclusion: Well-made.

Malibu Lime
21% ABV
✪
Colour/Nose: Overpowering, artificial lime.
Palate: Very sweet and confected; also a bit hollow in the centre.
Finish: Short, which for me is no bad thing.
Conclusion: Only available in Barbados.

Matusalem (USA)
Miami, Florida, USA
Founded in Cuba in the 1870s. Today the rums (a Caribbean blend) are produced in the Dominican Republic.
Tel: + 1 305 448 8255
Fax: + 1 305 445 1835
Website: www.matusalem.com

Matusalem Platino
40% ABV
✪✪✪(✪)
Colour/Nose: Bright. Buttery and soft, almost creamy with light citric notes, white chocolate.
Palate: Fat: masses of vanilla, crème caramel, lychee, apricot. Rounded, soft and creamy.
Finish: Soft.
Conclusion: A characterful, sweet, white rum.

Matusalem Clasico
40% ABV
✪✪✪
Colour/Nose: Gold. Dry with notes of peel.

Palate: Medium-bodied and very sweet, with a thick, silky feel. Melting vanilla ice-cream.
Finish: Gentle.
Conclusion: Well-made. A good cocktail rum.

Matusalem Gran Reserva Solera
✪✪✪(✪)
Colour/Nose: Light amber. Needs water to bring out coconut, vanilla, white pepper.
Palate: Very spicy, showing good wood-age, then that signature sweet vanilla character.
Finish: A little sugary.
Conclusion: The top of the Matusalem range.

La Mauny (Martinique)
Rivière Pilote, Martinique
An old sugar estate, La Mauny's rum activities began when it was bought by the Bellonnie brothers in 1920, though it wasn't fully marketed in France until 1977. Now distributed by Marie-Brizard.
Tel: + 596 596 56 82 82
Fax: + 596 596 56 82 83
Website: www.rhumdemartinique.com

La Mauny Blanc
50% ABV
✪✪(✪)
Colour/Nose: Light; crisp. Citric and floral.
Palate: Austere and dry. Touches of apricot.
Finish: Dry.
Conclusion: Clean and crisp.

Mount Gay (Barbados)
Part of Groupe Rémy-Cointreau
Brandons, St Michael, Barbados
Heritage stretches back to the start of sugar-making in Barbados. Mount Gay is a blend of pot and continuous still rums.
Tel: + 1 246 425 9066
Fax: + 1 246 425 8770
Website: www.mountgay.com

Mount Gay White
43% ABV
✪✪✪
Colour/Nose: Butter and vanilla. Floral with a touch of passion-fruit.

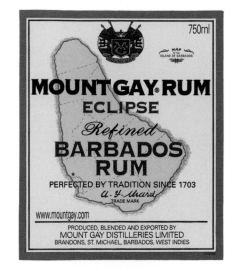

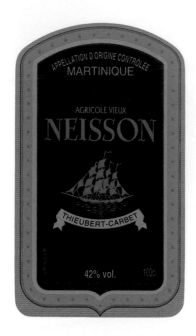

Palate: Clean, mellow. Sweet. Good balance.
Finish: Light.
Conclusion: Clean, well-made mixer.

Mount Gay White Overproof
74% ABV
✪✪✪(✪)

Colour/Nose: Pure with notes of light spice.
Floral and intense. Cane juice and hint of sweets.
Palate: Sweet and smooth. Mouth-watering.
Finish: Dry.
Conclusion: An overproof that doesn't neutralize
your taste-buds! Available only in Barbados.

Mount Gay Eclipse
40% ABV
✪✪✪✪

Colour/Nose: Light gold. Candy-floss sweetness,
vanilla, soft fruits, cherrry, walnut whip.
Palate: Very soft. Melting. Lightish but complex.
Finish: Creamy and smooth.
Conclusion: A great example of the balanced
Bajan style given some weight from the pot still.

Mount Gay Sugar Cane Brandy
40% ABV
✪✪✪(✪)

Colour/Nose: Gold. Fresh and very sweet:
toffee apple, lightly toasted oak. Lovely.
Palate: Round and sweet; hit of tropical fruits.
Finish: Dries nicely.
Conclusion: Worth seeking out.

Mount Gay Extra Old
43% ABV
✪✪✪✪✪

Colour/Nose: More obvious pot-still component
and maturity. Weighty with chocolate and oak,
fennel seed, tobacco, cashew nut, black banana.
Palate: Gentle, sweet, peachy fruits, then a richer
mid palate (dried fruits), then spice, then fruit.
Finish: Rich and full.
Conclusion: A perfect mature Barbadian style.

Mount Gay Tricentennial
40% ABV
✪✪✪✪(✪)

Colour/Nose: Powerful, complex, serious. Rich,
autumnal aromas: underbrush, mulch, truffle, fig

roll, chocolate. With water: into sherried territory
– dry amontillado. A classic aged spirit.
Palate: Rich, oaky, slightly tannic. Layers of old,
faded fruits.
Finish: Mighty, spicy, long.
Conclusion: A blend of (very) old rum made for
the 300th anniversary of the estate.

Neisson (Martinique)
Le Carbet, Martinique
Established in 1931, this small distillery
was nurtured by the remarkable Jean
Neisson: chemist, engineer, blender,
marketeer. It remains family owned.
Tel: + 596 596 78 03 70
Fax: + 596 596 78 03 95
Email: info@neisson.com
Website: www.neisson.com

Neisson Blanc
55% ABV
✪✪✪(✪)

Colour/Nose: Sweet. Filed with scents of cane
juice, red fruit, flowers. Rounded and soft.
Palate: Light with a clean, sweet, mid-palate.
Slight black-pepper tingle; light, passion-fruit.
Finish: Clean and soft.
Conclusion: Has lots of style.

Neisson Vieux
42% ABV
✪✪✪(✪)

Colour/Nose: Amber. Sweet with notes of
crème brûlée, prune (pruneaux d'Occitane),
cigar box. Similar to Armagnac. Generous.
Palate: Good toffee feel, with some dusty
tannin. Good balance and grip.
Finish: Soft, toffee-ish.
Conclusion: Richer, more opulent house style.

N.O. (USA)
Owned by Celebration
Distillation
New Orleans, Louisiana, USA
Created by artist/restaurateur James
Michaelopoulos, New Orleans rum is
waving a (slightly lonely) flag for rums

distilled in the mainland USA, and keeping up an old Louisianan tradition to boot.

Tel: + 00 1 504 945 9400
Email: info@neworleansrum.com
Website: www.neworleansrum.com

N.O. (New Orleans) Rum

43% ABV

✪✪✪

Colour/Nose: Amber. Smoky notes: roasted nut, black fruit, molasses. With water, an aroma of vanilla, tanned leather/saddles, and soot. Charred oak.
Palate: Sweet start, with maple syrup, nuts, and sweet oak.
Finish: Sooty.
Conclusion: Highly individualistic. Well-made.

Nutz & Rum Cream Liqueur

Owned by St Lucia Distillers
Castries, St Lucia

Another entry from St Lucia Distillers. This time: it's a peanut cream liqueur. (No, really…).

Tel: +758 451 4258
Fax: +758 451 4221
Email: info@sludistillers.com
Website: www.sludistillers.com

Nutz & Rum Cream Liqueur

20% ABV

✪✪✪

Colour/Nose: Gentle, with a hit like Brannigan's bar nuts (roasted peanuts with their skins still on) Fresh and natural.
Palate: Soft and not too sweet Peanut brittle.
Finish: Nutty and creamy.
Conclusion: Really good. Dangerously drinkable.

Old Oak

Part of Angostura/C.L. Global Brands
Port of Spain, Trinidad & Tobago
Tel: +868 623 1841/5
Fax: +868 623 1847
Email: icss@angostura.com
Website: www.angostura.com

Old Oak white

40% ABV

✪✪(✪)

Colour/Nose: Clean and light. Hint of soft fruit.
Palate: Soft and quite sweet. Delicate, clean.
Finish: Short but clean.
Conclusion: For the Trinidad market. A mixer.

Old Oak Gold

40% ABV

✪✪✪

Colour/Nose: Light but sugary: spices, young.
Palate: A good direct hit on the palate with some syrupy concentration. Crisps up nicely.
Finish: Clean.
Conclusion: Delicate and light as you'd imagine from Trinidad.

OVD (UK)

William Grant, Richmond, Surrey, UK

First produced by George Morton, a rum broker based in Montrose in the mid-nineteenth century, this Demerara blend remains a big seller in Scotland. Now part of Wm Grant's rum portfolio.

Tel: + 44 (0)208 332 1188
Fax: + 44 (0) 208 332 1695

OVD (Demerara blend)

40% ABV

✪✪(✪)

Colour/Nose: Treacle-dark. Very burnt, almost carbonized, nose reminiscent of sweet Madeira. Some black fruit and overripe banana.
Palate: Light- to medium-bodied with a fresh start, then the Madeira note appears. Big, fat, and warming.
Finish: Caramel.
Conclusion: You can see why this appeals in a cold northern climate.

Père Labat (Marie Galante)

Grand-Bourg, Marie Galante

From the island of Marie Galante, which lies off the coast of Guadeloupe.

Tel: + 590 97 93 42
Fax: +590 97 79 65

Père Labat Blanc

59% ABV

❍❍❍

Colour/Nose: Clear, bright. Rich, heavy and fruit-filled: white fruit, white peach. A big vegetal cane hit as well.

Palate: Sweet, with plenty of soft fruit: strawberry purée. Good texture.

Finish: Vegetal.

Conclusion: Powerful. Treat with respect.

Père Labat Paille

❍❍❍

Colour/Nose: Pale straw. Clean with dried grass, mint coconut, green banana.

Palate: Clean and quite sweet; has some dried spice, baked fruit, honey, and caramel mid-palate.

Finish: Soft.

Conclusion: Delicate. Well-made.

Père Labat Vieux

❍❍❍

Colour/Nose: Amber/copper with greenish rim. Old and mature: forest floor, walnut.

Palate: When neat, shows good balance between pretty rigid oak and toffee. Black fruits. Water, however, makes it highly tannic.

Finish: Oaky.

Conclusion: For lovers of very aged malt whiskies.

Pusser's (B.V.I.)

Tortola, B.V.I.

Rescued by former US marine Chuck Tobias when the British Navy finally abolished the daily rum ration. Blended in Tortola according to the original naval recipe, it has preserved a vital part of rum's heritage. The "pusser" was the officer who officiated at the daily ceremony.

Website: www.pussers.com

Pusser's British Navy Rum

(Caribbean blend)

54.5% ABV

❍❍❍(❍)

Colour/Nose: Mahogany. Rich with caramel toffee/toffee apple, cold tea, prune, dried roses. Water makes it sweeter with some leather.

Palate: Much sweeter than the nose suggests. Good impact of flavours, with sticky toffee rather than bitter caramel. Zingy yet sweet.

Finish: Spicy.

Conclusion: A classic.

Red Heart (UK/RSA)

Owned by Allied-Domecq
London, UK

Caribbean blend made by Allied-Domecq for the South African market, with higher percentage of Jamaican marks.

Tel: +44 (0) 20 7323 9000

Email: www.allieddomecqplc.com

Website: www.allieddomecqplc.com

Red Heart

40% ABV

❍❍❍

Colour/Nose: Mahogany/reddish glints. Lifted, quite pungent, higher-ester nose: banana, pear drop, vegetal.

Palate: Dry and quite crisp to start, then muscovado sugar, some dried pear and banana. Good balance.

Finish: Quite creamy.

Conclusion: Clean, lifted and quite punchy. A good blend.

Roaring Forties (New Zealand)

Owned by South Pacific Distillery
Nelson, New Zealand

New Zealand is a big rum-drinking nation, but traditionally had to rely on imported brands. Now it has a rum it can call its own.

Tel: + 64 3 546 6822

Fax: + 64 3 546 6826

Website: www.roaringforties.co.nz

Roaring Forties

40% ABV

❍❍❍(❍)

Colour/Nose: Reddish mahogany. Toasty with charred, roasted notes: liquorice sticks, molasses, leather, bitter chocolate. Heavy spirit.

Palate: Dark-chocolate aromas come through.

Finish: Short and clean.

Conclusion: Well-made, quite weighty spirit.
I'd like to see it with a bit more age.

Roaring Forties Overproof

57.5% ABV

✪✪✪

Colour/Nose: Light gold. Some singed
notes. Waxy. Young but with good weight.

Palate: Those attractive ash notes again.
Firm and hard with the higher alcohol.
Some sweetness.

Finish: Clean.

Conclusion: Powerful but well-made.

Ron Santiago de Cuba

Santiago de Cuba, Cuba

Tel: +53 22 2 5576

Ron Santiago de Cuba Añejo

38% ABV

✪✪

Colour/Nose: Amber. Light; a little insubstantial.

Palate: Very light: marzipan and nuts, chocolate
cake. Medium-bodied; quite woody. Doesn't have
the sweet, lightness of other Cuban brands.

Finish: Short, dry.

Conclusion: Another domestic Cuban brand.

Royal Oak (Trinidad)

Part of Angostura/C. L. Global Brands
Port of Spain, Trinidad & Tobago

Tel: +868 623 1841/5

Fax: +868 623 1847

Email: icss@angostura.com

Website: www.angostura.com

Royal Oak

40% ABV

✪✪✪✪

Colour/Nose: Mature, oaked notes moving
into almond, spices, and banana. Light
and sweet.

Palate: Fine but with central weight and some
richness from ripe fruits and sultana.

Finish: Soft.

Conclusion: Well-balanced.

Saint Etienne (Martinique)

Gros-Morne

Saint Etienne first appeared in 1909. It is
now produced at the Distillerie Simon.

Tel: + 596 596 57 62 68

Fax: + 596 596 57 54 11

Email: habitation.saint.etienne@wanadoo.fr

Saint Etienne Blanc

50% ABV

✪✪✪

Colour/Nose: Clear, bright. Light and juicy.
In the melon/mango camp. Some vegetal notes.

Palate: Rich and mouth-filling. Cane juice.
Quite a pungent attack.

Finish: Clean.

Conclusion: Rich. Well-made. Traditional.

Saint Etienne Vieux

50% ABV

✪✪✪

Colour/Nose: Amber. Aromatic and creamily
sweet. Vanilla and a light vegetal note.

Palate: Soft and round. Clean, red fruits with
light spices and tobacco.

Finish: Clean, light oak.

Conclusion: Good quality.

St James (Martinique)

Owned by Rémy-Cointreau
Ste-Marie, Martinique

One of Martinique's largest distilleries
which also produces the rum for the
J. Bally brand, among others.

Tel: + 596 596 69 50 39

Fax: +596 596 69 29 60

Email: RMSJCG@wanadoo.fr

Website: www.saintjames-rum.com

St James Blanc

50% ABV

✪✪✪

Colour/Nose: Clear. Bright. Floral and light
with a grainy note. Lychee and orchid.

Palate: Sweet. Cane juice, green apple; sweet
with a dusty feel. Light and good.

Finish: Soft.

Conclusion: Good ti punch material.

St James Paille

50% ABV

✪✪✪

Colour/Nose: Pale straw. Has sweet fruit along with edge: blanched almond, pencil shavings.
Palate: Clean, sound, a little dry. Fine and fresh.
Finish: Light, toasty wood.
Conclusion: Clean, well-made, approachable.

St James Ambre

45% ABV

✪✪✪(✪)

Colour/Nose: Amber (!) Still has vegetal notes of youth; fruity character with powdered lime.
Palate: Round, sweet. Light nuts. Quite chewy.
Finish: Soft.
Conclusion: Approachable.

St James Vieux

42% ABV

✪✪✪(✪)

Colour/Nose: Copper. Green glint. Quite dry. Cherry wood, polished oak, a little pruney.
Palate: Fine. Still seems quite young which gives it a middle good kick. Good grip as well.
Finish: Firm.
Conclusion: Well-balanced.

St James Hors d'Age

43% ABV

✪✪✪✪

Colour/Nose: Copper/amber. Some maturity: nutbowl, orange, crème brûlée. Soft and ripe.
Palate: Sweet, nice on tongue. Good fruit layers.
Finish: Sweet. caramel toffee.
Conclusion: A high-quality and reliable range.

Samba (Brazil)

Cooperativa da Cachaça
Minas Gerais, Brazil

A blend of cachaças from the region's top producers bottled by the local co-op.
Tel: + 55 31 3296 6709
Email: coop@coocachaça.com.br

Samba & Caña Cachaça

39% ABV

✪✪✪✪(✪)

Colour/Nose: Clear, bright. Wonderfully sweet heady aromas of banana,honey, mulled wine.
Palate: Wonderful spices come through along with baked banana.Good sweet mid-palate.
Finish: Dries nicely.
Conclusion: Really good. For killer caipirinhas.

San Miguel (Ecuador)

Owned by Desarrollo Agropecuario
Guayaquil, Ecuador

The country's main distiller is found in the cane fields of the Guayas River plain. The rums are matured in the mountains.
Tel: + 593 4 225 2789
Fax: + 593 4 225 0165
Website: www.ronsanmiguel.com

San Miguel Plata

37.5% ABV

✪✪(✪)

Colour/Nose: Lightly fruity, lemon/lime, sugared almonds. Very clean with dry notes.
Palate: Light, soft. Gently reveals sugary palate.
Finish: Dies a bit quickly.
Conclusion: A clean, well-made mixer.

San Miguel Oro (Ecuador)

37.5% ABV

✪✪

Colour/Nose: Gold. Nutty, dry grass and straw, lemon, and green banana.
Palate: More vanilla and banana split. Light and clean with a touch of crisp almond.
Finish: Short.
Conclusion: Again, meant for mixing.

San Miguel 5 Años (Ecuador)

37.5% ABV

✪✪✪(✪)

Colour/Nose: Very light gold. Leafy and floral; pear drops, then chocolate, cherries, and cream
Palate: Crisp to start; balancing lacy sweetness.
Finish: Soft and short.
Conclusion: A light style, but really charming.

San Miguel 7 Años

40% ABV

✪✪✪(✪)

Colour/Nose: Light gold. Delicate. Macadamia nut, baked banana, and lemon-butter icing.
Palate: Light; better structure than the 5 Años.
Finish: Soft. Medium length.
Conclusion: Delicate, sweet, soft and charming.

R. L. Seale (Barbados)

Owned by R. L. Seale
Foursquare Distillery, St Phillip, Barbados
Only Foursquare brand with Seale seal.
Tel: + 1 246 426 0334
Fax: + 1 246 436 6003
E-mail: rumfactory@sunbeach.net
Website: www.foursquarerum.com

R. L. Seale's 10yo

40% ABV
✪✪✪✪✪

Colour/Nose: Elegant, mature notes: figgy, with a lifted bergamot note. Complex, rich but sexy.
Palate: Starts with cinnamon, then soaked raisin, dried peach, candied peel.
Finish: Cinnamon and treacle toffee.
Conclusion: Reminiscent of a hot summer day: flowers, the wood around you creaking in the heat.

Sea Wynde (USA)

Owned by Great Spirits
Rego Park, New York, USA
Named after a nineteenth-century Atlantic clipper. A blend of five pot-still rums from aged stocks held in Jamaica, Guyana, and the UK.
Tel: + 1 718 533 7717
Fax: +1 718 533 7610
Email: info@ greatspirits.com
Website: www.greatspiritscom.com

Sea Wynde

46% ABV
✪✪✪(✪)

Nose: Copper/amber. Intense and quite oily. Pungent Jamaican lift. Smoky, cherry, burnt orange peel, fruit cake, raisins. Soft yet intense.
Palate: Thick; mead-like. Smoky, coffee, red peppercorns, maraschino, peach, and marzipan.

Finish: Powerful, slightly smoky.
Conclusion: Big and robust. Sweet and bitter. Has power rather than finesse.

Tortuga (Cayman Islands)

Owned by the Tortuga Rum Co.
George Town, Grand Cayman
Based in the Cayman Islands since 1984, Tortuga is a blend of (predominantly) Jamaican and Bajan rums which are assembled at the firm's Tortugan base. They also make a wonderful rum cake.
Tel: + 354 949 7701/7867
Fax: + 354 949 6322
Email: tortuga@candw.ky
Website: www.tortugarums.com

Tortuga Light (Caribbean blend)

40% ABV
✪✪

Colour/Nose: Soft and light with orange and cashew nut notes. Dusty.
Palate: Rounded and slightly dry. Nutty, clean, and pleasant. As the name says. light.
Finish: Dry.
Conclusion: Clean spirit and well-enough made. Not hugely exciting, though.

Tortuga Gold

40% ABV
✪✪

Colour/Nose: Old gold. Round, with honey; weighty with a slight estery lift. Little hard.
Palate: Clean with good bite on the palate. Banana. Spirit seems young.
Finish: Little hard again.
Conclusion: A little unbalanced.

Tortuga Dark

40% ABV
✪✪

Colour/Nose: Mahogany/red. Lots of burnt toffee and raisins.
Palate: Thick and sweet, like Christmas cake. Burnt toffee.
Finish: Slightly bitter edge.
Conclusion: For lovers of old-style dark rums.

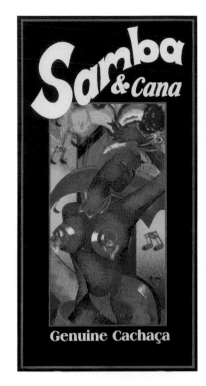

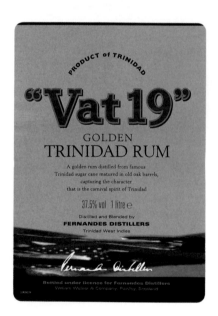

Tortuga Banana

30% ABV

✿

Colour/Nose: Gold. Green banana/banana skin notes. A slightly earthy, sappy tone.

Palate: Artificial and slightly hot.

Finish: Thin and dry.

Conclusion: Hard spirit, poorly covered up.

Tortuga Coconut

30% ABV

✿

Colour/Nose: Light gold. Raw spirit on top of coconut husk and flesh.

Palate: Hot and quite dry, with a greasy feel.

Finish: Hard.

Conclusion: Poor-quality spirit base lets down.

Trois Rivières (Martinique)

Ste-Luce, Martinique

An estate-grown rum located on some of the richest agricultural land in Martinique, Trois Rivières is now part of the same group which owns La Mauny.

Tel: + 596 596 56 82 82

Fax: + 596 596 56 82 83

Website: www.rhumdemartinique.com

Trois Rivières Blanc

50% ABV

✿✿(✿)

Colour/Nose: Quite fragrant. Oily with water.

Palate: Dry, with a slightly dusty feel. Clean with a mellow mid-palate.

Finish: Nutty.

Conclusion: Clean and crisp.

Ron Varadero (Cuba)

Distributed by Cimez

Lesser known than Havana Club, Cuba's second-biggest brand is also beginning to appear on European markets.

Tel: + 53 7 204 2126/204 0774

Fax: + 53 7 204 1996

E-mail: elastra@cimex.com.cu

Ron Varadero 3 Años

38% ABV

✿✿✿

Colour/Nose: Very pale yellow. Attractive, rounded, and sugary with a slight mintiness.

Palate: Medium-dry with life and bite on the mid-palate, then a lovely caramelized fruit edge.

Finish: Clean, rounded finish; a touch of coffee.

Conclusion: Great cocktail base.

Ron Varadero 5 Años

38% ABV

✿✿✿(✿)

Colour/Nose: Old gold. Light, almost lean, and delicate with musky notes: spices, marzipan, coconut, aniseed twists, spiced honey, ginger.

Palate: Rounded with some complexity. Citrus fruits then sweet, caramelized, exotic, tropical fruits. Rich, flavoursome, and perfumed with cinnamon, honey, and a dry streak all giving good structure.

Finish: Light.

Conclusion: Young with intriguing complexity. Great for cocktails. Watch out for this brand.

Ron Varadero Añejo

38% ABV

✿✿(✿)

Colour/Nose: Dark amber. Soft, gentle, easy-going, but seems to lack any great definition.

Palate: Good balance between crisp spiciness and soft sweet fruitiness.

Finish: A slightly short finish.

Conclusion: Decent mid-palate sweetness; doesn't quite hang together.

Vat 19 (Trinidad)

Caribbean: Angostura, Port of Spain, Trinidad & Tobago

Europe: Wm. Grant, Surrey, UK

Trinidadian brand, first produced by Fernandes and now by Angostura.

Tel: +868 623 1841/5

Fax: +868 623 1847

Email: icss@angostura.com

Website: www.angostura.com

Tel: + 44 (0)208 332 1188

Fax: + 44 (0) 208 332 1695

Vat 19 Golden Rum

37.5% ABV

○○○

Colour/Nose: Old gold. Clean and attractive. Perfumed: guava/mango. Delicate spicy smoke.
Palate: Light and delicate. Starts sweetly before the toasted spices appear, then guava, mango.
Finish: Clean and dry.
Conclusion: A charming, sweet mixer. A 40% ABV version is sold in Trinidad which has slightly better grip on the palate.

Wood's (UK)

Owned by Wm. Grant
Richmond, Surrey, UK
Another ex-Seagram rum which has been a solid performer on the UK dark rum market for years.
Tel: + 44 (0)208 332 1188
Fax: + 44 (0) 208 332 1695

Wood's 100 Old Navy Rum

57% ABV

○○(○)

Colour/Nose: Very dark-brown. Tarry. Sweet and concentrated. Coffee and cream with water.
Palate: Sweet and thick: black banana. Camp coffee with nutty sweetness before the finish.
Finish: Sweet.
Conclusion: A well-made example of its style, but a little one-dimensional.

Wray & Nephew (Jamaica)

Spanish Town, Jamaica
Firm of John Wray and nephew, Charles Ward. Started life when Wray opened a rum shop in Kingston in 1825. By 1862 (with Ward), Wray had started blending rums, and by the start of the twentieth century had begun to buy sugar estates and distilleries including Appleton. Today, the company has two distilleries. Overproof is THE iconic Jamaican brand.
Tel: +876 963 9215/6/7
Fax: +876 963 9218
Email: appleton@infochan.com
Website: www.appletonrum.com

Wray & Nephew White Overproof Rum

63% ABV

○○○○○

Colour/Nose: Clear, bright. A rounded, rich nose with ripe banana, molasses, lime, and a touch of cashew. Has real substance. Good, clean spirit.
Palate: Ripe. Showing notes of banana, grass, nuts, and sweetness. That cashew note keeps things crisp while the richness of the spirit stops it just vapourizing in the mouth.
Finish: Grassy and long.
Conclusion: The best overproof on the market. Punchy but classy.

Zacapa (Guatemala)

Owned by Industrias Licoreras de Guatemala, Guatemala City
Large distiller making all of Guatemala's rums, although original distillery brand names, such as Zacapa, have been retained. Centenario is a *solera*-aged rum.
Tel: + 502 597 9979
Fax: + 502 597 9995
Website: www.industrias-licoreras.com

Zacapa Centenario

40% ABV

○○○○(○)

Colour/Nose: Ruby red to copper. Sweetly complex to start: notes of chestnut, honey, morello cherry, chocolate, peels, smoky wood, and dried tarragon. Then becomes savoury: tobacco, grilled nuts, leather… even creosote, and with water, an aroma like incense.
Palate: Sweet all the way. Mouth-coating. Cherry sweets, molasses. Hugely concentrated.
Finish: Sugary.
Conclusion: A huge, impressive, showy rum.

Bibliography

The following are the major titles I have consulted in the writing of this book. If you are interested in reading more on rum, I can heartily recommend the works of Edward Thompson and Luis Ayala.

Arroyo, Rafael. "Studies on Rum", *Research Bulletin No.5.* San Juan PR: University of Puerto Rico Agricultural Experiment Station, 1945.

Asbury, Herbert. *The Great Illusion: an Informal History of Prohibition*, New York: Doubleday, 1950.

Ayala, César. *American Sugar Kingdom.* Chapel Hill NC: University of North Carolina Press, 1999.

Ayala, Luis. *The Rum Experience.* Rum Runner Press, www.rumshop.net: 2001.

Ayala, Luis. *The 2002/3 Rum Buyer's Guide.* www.rumshop.net: 2002.

Barty-King, Hugh, & Massel, Anton. *Rum Yesterday and Today.* London: Heinemann, 1983.

Beachey RW. *The British West Indian Sugar Industry in the late 19th century.* Oxford: 1957.

Bonera, Miguel. *Oro Blanco: Una Historia Empresarial de Ron Cubano (Tomo 1).* Toronto: Lugus Libros Latin America, 2000.

Brathwaite, Edward Kamau. "Mother Poem", Oxford: Oxford University Press, 1977.

Brown, John Hull. *Early American Beverages.* Rutland VT: Charles E. Tuttle, 1966.

Burrowes, John. *On the Manufacture of Rum and Spirits.* Georgetown: Guiana Planters Assoc., 1876.

Camard-Hayot, Florette, & de Lagaurigue Jean-Luc. *Martinique, Terre de Rhum.* Bordeaux: Traces, 1997.

Campoamor, Fernando. *El Hijo Alegre de la Caña de Azúcar.* Havana: Editorial Cientifico-Tecnica, 1993.

Cooper, A. *The Complete Distiller.* London: 1757.

de la Casas, Bartholome. *Historia de las Indias.* Mexico City: Fondo de Cultura Economica, 1951.

Deren, Maya. *The Voodoo Gods.* St Albans: Paladin, 1975.

Devaux, Robert. *Industrial History of Roseau.* St Lucia: private publication, 1997.

Dillon, Patrick. *The Much Lamented Death of Madam Genever.* London: Review, 2002.

Embury, David. *The Fine Art of Mixing Drinks.* New York: Doubleday, 1958.

Exquemelin, Alexander. *The Buccaneers of America.* New York: Dover Publications, 2000.

Grimes, William. *Straight Up or on the Rocks.* New York: North Point Press, 2001.

Haddock, Daniel, Hernandez, Leslie (and others). *La Industria Ron en Puerto Rico 1937–1948.* Puerto Rico: University of Puerto Rico Agricultural Experiment Station, 1956.

Hamilton, Edward. *The Complete Guide to Rum.* Chicago: Triumph, 1997.

Harrison, Michelle. *King Sugar* London: Latin American Bureau, 2001.

Hoarau, Michel. *Le Rhum a l'Ile de la Réunion.* La Réunion: 2001.

Huetz de Lemps, Alain. *Histoire du Rhum.* Paris: Editions Desjonqueres, 1997.

Jacques, K.A., and Lyons, T.P. Kelsall D.R. (eds). *The Alcohol Textbook (3rd edition).* Nottingham: Nottingham University Press, 2001.

James, C.L.R. *The Black Jacobins*. London: Penguin, 1980.

Knight, Franklin. *The Caribbean: Genesis of a Fragmented Nationalism*. Oxford: Oxford University Press, 1990.

Kobler John. *Ardent Spirits*. New York: Da Kapo, 1993.

Père Labat. *Memoires des Nouveaux Voyages faits aux Iles Francaises de l'Amerique*. [Facsimile edition.] London: Frank Cass, 1970.

Laurie, Peter. *The Barbadian Rum Shop*. Oxford: Macmillan Caribbean, 2001.

Leroy, Eric. *Images du Rhum*. Martinique: Gondwana editions, 1996.

Lewisholm, Florence. *Divers Information on The Romantic History of St Croix*. St Croix: St. Croix Landmarks Society, 1964.

Ligon, Richard. *A True and Exact History of the Island of Barbadoes*. [Facsimile edition.] London: Frank Cass, 1998.

Mill, John Stuart. *Principles of Political Economy (Book 2)*. New York: Kelley, 1995.

Mintz, Stanley. *Sweetness and Power*. New York: Penguin, 1986,

Missen, François (and others). *Cuba: The Legend of Rum*. Toulouse: Editions Bahia Presse, (publication date unknown).

Monge, José Trias. *Puerto Rico: The Trials of the oldest Colony in the World*. New Haven, New Haven, 1997.

Pack, James, Captain. *Nelson's Blood*. Annapolis: Naval Institute Press, 1983.

Pepin, Anabel García. *Ron en Puerto Rico: Tradicion y Cultura*. Puerto Rico: Rums of Puerto Rico, 2002.

Phillips, Caryl. *A New World Order*. London: Secker & Warburg, 2001.

Phillips, Caryl. *The Atlantic Sound*. London: Vintage, 2000.

Regan, Gary, & Regan, Mardee Haidin. *New Classic Cocktails*. New York: Macmillan, 1997.

Smith, Adam. *Wealth of Nations*. Oxford: Oxford University Press, 1998.

Taussig, Charles. *Rum, Romance and Rebellion*. London: Jarrolds, (publication date unknown).

Thomas, Jerry. *Bartender's Guide*. [Facsimile edition.] Angouleme: Vintagebook, 2001.

Thompson, Peter. *Rum Punch and Revolution*. Philadelphia: University of Philadelphia Press, 1999.

Torres, Calixta. *Know Your Rum*. Puerto Rico: University of Puerto Rico Agricultural Experiment Station, (publication date unknown).

Author unknown. *The Barman's Sixth Sense*. Budapest: Interpress, 1980.

Author unknown. *The Distiller of London*. 1639.

Walcott, Derek. *Collected Poems*, London: Faber & Faber, 1992.

Walcott, Derek. *Omeros*. London: Faber & Faber, 1990.

Warner, Jessica. *Craze: Gin and Debauchery in an Age of Reason*. London: Profile, 2003.

Williams, Eric. *Capitalism and Slavery*. Chapel Hill NC: University of North Carolina Press, 1994.

Williams, Eric. *From Columbus to Castro: The History of the Caribbean 1492–1969*. London: Andre Deutsch, 1970.

Index

Acknowledgments

This book could not have been written without the help of a number of people.

Extra special thanks should go to the distillers and blenders who not only spared their valuable time in showing me how their rums were made but kindly answered all my secondary questions and then read my copy to ensure no mistakes were made: Ben Cross de Chavannes (Main Rum), Bill Edwards (Cruzan), Jerry Edwards (Mount Gay), Steve Hoyles (Allied-Domecq), Alty McKenzie (Appleton), George Robinson (D.D.L.), Richard Seale (Foursquare) and Carsten Vlierboom (E. & A. Scheer).

Particular thanks to: Reglita Jimenez (Havana Club), Giselle Laronde-West (Angostura), Catherine McDonald (Wray & Nephew), and Emmanuel Becheau (Clément/J.M.) for superb planning and organization which allowed Jason and me to get the fullest possible picture of your countries.

Thanks also to: Joy Spence and Tania Marley (Wray & Nephew) Alton James, the best taxi driver in MoBay; Juan-Carlos Gonzalez Delgado, Yolanda Perez, Ranses Villar, Stefano Oldrati and Jorge (Havana Club) and all the bartenders we pestered in Havana. Viva Cuba!; Robyn Gollop-Knight, Rosma Baird and Peter Marshall (Mount Gay); Jo-anne Pooler (W.I.R.D.); Philip Mayers (Cockspur); David Ellis; Laurie Barnard, Michael Speakman, Katherine Felix and all at St Lucia Distillers; Patrik Goasdoué and Anne Pes (Clément); Jean-Myrtil Laurent (Rémy Caribbean); Bernard Bain, Rose-May Narayansingh, Anne-Marie Ramdhan, John Georges, Patrick Patel, Peter Traboulay, Gabriel Faria, and Alex (Angostura/C.L.); Joyce Abdul (Caroni); Yesu Persaud (D.D.L.); Guillermo Garcia-Lay (Bacardi); Kristyn Monrose (Clarke's Court); Gary Nelthropp and Tom Valdes (Cruzan); Wanda Lugo and Dr. Alberto Pantoja (U.P.R.); Pastora Bermúdez; Arnaud de Trabuc and Thierry Gardère (Barbancourt); Alvaro Martínez Salvo and Claudia Monserrat (Flor de Caña); Roque Chavez (San Miguel); Anant Kanoi (Nepal Distillers) and Abby O'Neil for last minute tracking down.

In the USA, thanks go to: Kendal Anderson and Erin Houchin (Edelman), Malcolm Atherton (Real Rum), Anitra Budd (Ketchum) and Gary Regan.

Closer to home, big thanks to: Geoff Adams (Jefferson's); John Barrett, Tom Jago (Bristol Spirits); Henry Butler (Brighton's best wine merchant); Simon Chase (Hunters & Frankau); Charlotte Fraser (Richmond Towers); Su-Lin Ong, David Hume (Wm Grant); Lindsay Clelland (Grosvenor Brands); Akos Forzek; Ranald MacDonald (Boisdale); Bertrand Lienafa; Peter Martin and John Hammond (Wray & Nephew); Neil Mathieson (Eaux de Vie); Nick Morgan (Diageo); Sukhinder Singh; David Stirk (Cadenhead); Vanessa Wright (Chivas Bros.); Danny, Brian, Tuula, Tom and the rest of the Havana crew "Never Get Off the Boat!"; Nick Strangeway; Asa, J.D. and Dale at Match.

Thanks also to Susy Atkins, Andrew Jefford, and Charlie MacLean for morale-boosting support.

At Mitchell Beazley, immense thanks to Hilary for bearing with me over the first frustrating few months and being an always understanding, patient and supportive editor. We did it! To Jamie for superb editing and to Emma for doing all those tedious but necessary jobs without complaint.

A huge thank you to Jason for being not just a great photographer but a perfect travelling companion and friend.. "Later..."

Lastly, to my wife Jo who has somehow yet again managed to put up with my demented behaviour during the writing of another book and who has borne my prolonged absences, rants, moods, and the fact that the house is filled with bottles with astounding good humour. I couldn't have done it without your loving support.